"I Didn't Get to Say Goodbye, Now What Can I Do?"

Practical Tools to Learn Manage the
Pain, Anger and Sorrow of Not Achieving Closure with a
Loved One and Start Living a Well Balanced, Peaceful and
Content Life

Includes the Book - Part Two:

Write Your Own Funeral Service

Prepare and Deliver Your Own
Funeral Service/Celebration of Life for
Family Members, Friends and
Loved Ones That Were Not Able to Receive a Proper
Burial Service

Rev. Oreste J. D'Aversa

PUBLISHER'S NOTE

This book is designed to provide accurate and authoritative. Information in regard to the subject matter covered. It is sold with the understanding that neither the author nor publisher is engaged in rendering psychological, legal, or other professional service. If psychological, legal, professional advice or other expert assistance is required, the services of a professional, in that field should be sought. The principles and concepts presented in this book are the opinions of the author and based on his interpretations of the aforementioned principles. Neither the author nor publisher is liable or responsible to any person or entity for any errors contained on this book, website, or for any special, incidental, or consequential damage caused or alleged to be caused directly or indirectly by the information contained on this book or website. Any application of the techniques, ideas and suggestions in this book is at the reader's sole discretion and risk.

Copyright © Oreste J. D'Aversa, 2022. All rights reserved.

No part of this publication may be reproduced, redistributed, taught, stored in a retrieval system, or transmitted, in any form, or by any means, electronic, mechanical, photocopy, recording, or otherwise, without the prior written permission of the publisher.

FIRST EDITION

ISBN: 978-1-952294-16-7

Library of Congress Control Number: 2021925078

Published by: Cutting Edge Technology Publishing

Part One (Book):
TABLE OF CONTENTS

About the Author	9
Introduction	15
Chapter 1: YOU are Important	23
Chapter 2: Meditation: Centering Yourself in Mind, Body and Spirit	29
Chapter 3: Reaching Out Through Writing Letters	37
Chapter 4: Guided Imagery: A Useful Tool in Healing	43
Chapter 5: Mediumship: Fact or Fiction	57
Chapter 6: Connecting with Nature	71
Chapter 7: GOD Told Me to Tell You You're Not Alone	77
Conclusion	87
Footnotes	91
Bibliography	93
Grief Resources	95

THIS PAGE INTENTIONALLY LEFT BLANK

Part Two (Book):

Write Your Own Funeral Service

Prepare and Deliver Your Own
Funeral Service/Celebration of Life for
Family Members, Friends and
Loved Ones That Were Not Able to Receive a Proper
Burial Service

TABLE OF CONTENTS

1. About the Author — 115

2. Introduction — 117

3. Memorial Service — 121

4. Funeral Prayers/Quotes — 163

5. Conclusion — 215

6. Worksheets — 219

7. Footnotes — 261

8. Bibliography — 267

THIS PAGE INTENTIONALLY LEFT BLANK

Dedication

I dedicate this book to all people that have lost a loved ones unexpectedly.

May this book help soften the pain that you are experiencing, help start you on your healing journey and may you begin to find peace in your heart.

Know that GOD is with you every step of the way offering you guidance, protection, and love.

THIS PAGE INTENTIONALLY LEFT BLANK

About the Author

Rev. Oreste J. D'Aversa, "Reverend Rusty" as he is known informally, is an Inter-Faith (All-Faiths) Minister ordained by The New Seminary in New York City, New York.

He believes in the teachings of God, Jesus Christ, the Prophets, and the Ascended Masters. He is here to serve God and humankind to help make the world a better place for all people.

Reverend D'Aversa is an Author, Public Speaker, Spiritual Coach/Advisor and helps people find their true life's purpose and spiritual path. He is also a Business Coach, Consultant, Trainer and University Lecturer. He has appeared on radio and television as well as having his work featured in various newspapers and journals.

He is author of the following books:

- **Life Beyond the Pandemic:**

A Practical New Journey Handbook

- **SELLING for NON-SELLING Professionals**

- **Baby Boomer Entrepreneur**

(All available on Amazon.com)

His websites:

www.GodLovesYouAndMe.org

www.LifeBeyondThePandemic.com

www.MetroSmallBusinessCoaching.com

He can be reached at:

Email: OresteDAversa@outlook.com

Preface

One of the main reasons I wrote this book was how I was and am deeply sadden as an Inter-Faith (All-Faiths) Minister (and as a regular person) by all the lost souls of September 11 and other world-wide tragedies that so many people are emotionally suffering by not having had the chance to say goodbye to a loved one or multiple loved ones. Yet another example of life not being fair, it is emotionally painful for all those involved none the less. Same people may say, "It has been X amount of time since your loved one(s) have died, isn't time you got over it and moved on? Emotions are emotions, you feel what you feel, for as long as you feel them – it may even be a lifetime that you feel and carry the emotional pain of losing a loved one(s).

This book is not to take the place of working with trained health care, mental health professionals and spiritual professionals but can be used "in addition to and not instead of" working with trained bereavement professionals, support groups and others that assist you in your bereavement and healing process.

This book is designed to give you additional tools in your "Healing Journey Toolbox" for your healing journey. As previously mentioned I am an Inter-Faith (All-Faiths) Minister I have studies many religions and spiritual traditions, some of that knowledge is in this book regarding what happens to all of us when we transition (die). **I ask that you keep an open mind and remember that the information in this book is meant to be used "in addition to and not instead of" your religious and spiritual beliefs and practices.** Use the tools in this book that resonate with you, that you feel can and will help you on your healing journey. As the saying goes, "keep what you like and leave the rest."

May this book help you find peace in your heart and in your soul for the loved one(s) you have lost. Let the grace of GOD always be upon you.

THIS PAGE INTENTIONALLY LEFT BLANK

Introduction

Losing a loved one(s) even when you know they are dying and going to die is painful at best, losing a loved one without warning is devastation at it worst. All of your body goes into shock – physically, mentally, emotionally, and spiritually. Life does not make sense anymore. You are thrown instantly into situations that need to be handled immediately, from the basic things of canceling social engagements to the most important, complex, and emotionally frighting realities as planning funeral, wills and estates and going home to an empty house that no longer feels like a home.

The purpose of this book is not to relive the unpleasantries of the lose of a loved one(s) but rather to give you additional tools on your healing journey, in the hopes one day, to start moving on with your life once again. The tools in this book are not meant to have you forget the memories of your loved one(s) but rather have you remembered your loved one(s) in a loving, caring, and emotionally healthy manner. You want to be in control of those memories and not have the memories control you. You want to know, acknowledge, and understand that you are a better person for knowing your loved one(s) and realize that your loved one(s) were in your life whether for a specific reason, season, or a lifetime their work on this earthly plane is completed and they have moved on to do their next journey in their soul's evolution as you are meant to move on to do the next chapter in your soul's journey in your own life and evolution.

In this chapter, there will be an overview of each chapter that will be discussed in this book and to prepare the reader for the tools being presented. It is asked that you, the reader have and **keep an open mind to the subject matter discussed,** as it may be new and/or go against teachings that the reader has been raised on or teaching that were misinterpreted by the media, rumors in society, gossip that is incorrect or just plain ignorance of the subject matter at hand. Keeping an open mind will allow for more possibilities for the healing journey of people that have suddenly lost loved one(s).

In **Chapter 1: YOU Are Important** is about taking time for yourself after experiencing such a traumatic event as losing a loved one(s). Starting the journey back to "Wholeness" by starting to add to the collection of tools in your "Healing Toolbox" by "Creating Sacred Space for Yourself" and starting to allow yourself the gift of opening yourself up to let all of your feeling out with another tool "Your Journal: "Your Spiritual Confidante".

Chapter 2 – Meditation: Centering Yourself in Mind, Body and Spirit you will learn "What is Mediation?", "How Can Meditation Help Me?", the "Types of Meditation: Self-Directed and Guided Meditation" and you will learn a simple yet powerful exercise to learn mediation "Meditate Every Day: The Simple Yet Powerful – One-Two-Three Method of Meditation". This exercise is especially good for people who think they cannot shut off their minds from thinking and people that feel they cannot learn meditation. Do it for 30 days morning and night and watch your life be transformed in a positive way!

In **Chapter 3: Reaching Out Through Writing Letters** you will learn the importance writing letters to help you release whatever needs to said to your departed loved one(s) that may or may not have in said while they were alive. Your will learn more about this in the section called:

"Why Write Letters to the Departed?". Also what will be discussed in this chapter are "Sample Topics to Write About" and "What to Do with The Letters After You Write Them?". The exercise for this chapter is to "Write Letters to Your Departed Loved Ones".

Chapter 4: Guided Imagery: A Useful Tool in Healing will teach you another useful tool in your healing journey. In this chapter you will learn: "What is Guide Imagery?" and "How Can Guided Imagery Help Me?". The exercise in this chapter is an "Example of a Guided Imagery Exercise in Connecting with a Departed Loved One" which you may want to record (or have someone else record it for you) and play it to yourself in the quietness and sanctity of your sacred space (not while driving).

In **Chapter 5: Mediumship: Fact or Fiction** you will learn about Mediumship that working with a Medium can be another useful tool in your healing journey. You will learn;

- "What is a Medium and Mediumship?"
- "Why Work with a Medium?"
- "Should _YOU_ Work with a Medium?"
- "Mediumship and Religion"
- "The Use of Mediums: Point and Counter-Point then You Decide"
- "What to Look For When Working with a Medium"
- Example of a Working Medium – Elizabeth Rose
- Exercise: Prepare Questions for Your Reading with a Medium

Chapter 6: Connecting with Nature learn the importance of spending time with nature in your healing journey.

Read about:

- Why Nature is So Important?
- Nature Your Other Sacred Space
- Getting Closer to God While in Nature
- Exercise: Spend Time in Nature

In Chapter 7: God Told Me to Tell You You're Not Alone. You will understand that while at times you may feel alone in truth you never are really alone. Learn and get more tools about the following:

- Why Go to God?
- The Power of Prayer
- Prayers for the Departed
- Exercise: Prayer and Meditation

In the **Conclusion**, there will a summary and wrap up of all things discussed in the entire book.

THIS PAGE INTENTIONALLY LEFT BLANK

Chapter 1: YOU Are Important

Take time for YOU

It's very important that while on your healing journey you take time for yourself. The stress of losing a loved one(s) impacts us and our bodies on all levels – physically, mentally, emotionally, and spiritually, so it's important to remember that while we are talking care of the tasks that happen with the death of an individual it is just as important to take care of yourself.

In taking care of yourself you want to do it on all levels of your being – Physically (The Body) by eating right, exercising to the degree that make sense in your life and getting plenty of rest. Mentally (The Mind) by listening and putting positive things in your mind through this challenging time in your life, by not listening to much negativity by watching the news, being around negative people, etc. Emotionally (The Emotional Heart) during a time of grieving it may be hard to give or be of service to others, but it may be a good to nurture yourself. Spending time with animals it a good way to do this as they are such givers of love with having no expectations in return. Whether you have an animal or not there are always animal shelters and adoption centers in most towns to volunteer or just visit and spend time with the animals there. Both you and the animals will feel better for doing so. And Spiritually (The Life Force), do something that will lift your spirit up. Pray, meditate, spend time in nature. Unplug your mind and recharge your inner being and do it on a daily basis, you'll thank yourself for doing so.

Create Sacred Space for Yourself

Let's start off with what is "Sacred Space". The word sacred is usually reserved for holy places. Sacred space is found in all the major religions of the world. Such a space can be a church, a synagogue, temple, a mosque, a cathedral, or a being in nature. Sacred space does not require a building or trees. It can be any quiet, space that connects you to GOD or to what is meaningful in your life. It is a space conducive to meditation, prayer, or quiet contemplation.

Though there are no rules, regulations or plans on how to create sacred space. **Altars** tend to be a common theme in most sacred spaces as they provide a physical representation of spiritual intention. Rituals and ceremonies are common exercises performed in sacred space; the lighting of a candle(s), the burning of incense, flowers and/or objects that have meaning to a person. Your sacred space should be a place of quiet reflection and help provide you with a level of spiritual comfort.

Find a quiet place in your home where you can create some sacred space. If you do not have any items, you can usually find everything you need at home, in local stores and there is always online shopping that will even provide with a "Altar in a Box" to get you started.

Your Journal: Your Spiritual Confidante

What is journaling and how can it help you you're your healing? Journaling is writing down your thoughts and feelings to help you understand them more clearly. It is a place (the journal) where you can write all of your thoughts and feelings. Uncensored, not having to be concerned about what other people are thinking or saying about your thoughts and emotions.

There are proven benefits of journaling some of which are:
- help to reduce stress
- helps manage anxiety and depression
- give you an opportunity for self-discovery

- self-realization and spiritual growth.

You can write out all of your thoughts, feelings, and emotions in a private journal that you re-read what you have written and ponder upon what you have written. Your journal is a "no judgement zone" for you, by you and for you and your personal reflection on your life and what you are going through – the good and sometimes the not so good.

Exercises: Create Scared Space and Start Journaling.

a. Create Scared Space. Find a place in your bedroom, house or on your property where you can create your own personal sacred space and create your alter. Bring items on your alter that are important, special and have meaning to you.

b. Start Journaling. Go to a store and buy yourself a blank lined diary and start writing. The diary does not have to be fancy or expensive, it can be a blank composition book that can usually be purchased for less than a dollar. The most important thing is that you start writing as soon as possible. Whether you feel happy, sad, or just indifferent – start writing now!

Chapter 2: Meditation: Centering Yourself in Mind, Body and Spirit

What is Meditation?

Mediation is defined by Wikipedia as, "Meditation is a practice where an individual uses a technique – such as mindfulness, or focusing the mind on a particular object, thought, or activity – to train attention and awareness, and achieve a mentally clear and emotionally calm and stable state. Meditation is practiced in numerous religious traditions." I personally believe it to be the alignment of the Physical (the Body), the Mental (the Mind), the Emotional (the Emotional Heart) and Spiritual (the Life Force with us) and by meditating you are creating a feeling of calm and wellbeing for yourself.

How Can Meditation Help Me?

Our minds are one of the most powerful tools we have as human beings. Yet we are not taught how to use the mind to its full potential. Furthermore, the irony is we are using our minds more in modern times and our physical bodies less and yet there are few teachings about how to utilize our minds properly, as well as how to rest our minds in a world full of all types of stressors, bad news and anxiety producing events.

Most "dis-ease" starts in the mind due to the stress and anxiety of modern day living (job/career stress, family issues, personal relationships, deaths and dying, etc.). The losing of a loved one(s) is stressful enough let alone losing a loved one(s) unexpectedly and compounding the situation if the loved one(s) were lost in a sudden and tragic manner. Meditation is a practical tool that you can use immediately to help deal with the stress of having lost loved one(s) in your life, as well as dealing with the stress in both your professional and personal life.

Types of Meditation:
Self-Directed and Guided Meditation

While there are many meditation techniques (which you are encouraged to research and learn about), they basically boil down to two methods either:

- **Self-Directed.** Using the Self-Directed Method as stated, you are doing the meditation yourself as the example being presented to you in the next section in this chapter where you are directing yourself using a meditation technique, no outside equipment, person, or anything else is required. You can perform the meditation, any time, any place (**not while driving or performing any focused activity**) and go into a deep state of meditation all on your own.

- **Guided Meditation.** While the Guided Meditation Method, you are being guided by a person, a recording, or other means where you are listening to a person giving you instruction. The down part about Guided Meditation Method is that you need to have access to a person, recording or things outside of yourself to do the meditation.

Though I prefer the Self-Directed Method myself because I can do it anytime, anyplace, and anywhere (not while driving), especially if I just left an extremely stressful situation both methods are good and helpful for health and mental wellbeing.

Exercise: Meditate Every Day

The Simple Yet Powerful – One-Two-Three Method of Meditation

Meditation is aligning **Mind, Body, Emotions and Spirit**, so that these components function as one. Meditating is the practice of quieting the mind of all its chatter to enable you to be open to the thoughts of the Universe.

The benefit of this exercise is to become centered in oneself.

1. This is the **"1 – 2 – 3 – 4" Method of Meditation**.

2. Take a slow deep **breath in** for a count up to four – one, two, three, four.

3. Then slowly **exhale out** for a count up to four – one, two, three, four.

4. Take a total of 3 or 4 slow deep breaths.

5. Then just say to yourself, in your mind, **"1 – 2 – 3 – 4"** over and over again.

6. The purpose of this is to focus your mind on the counting and away from the chatter that is with us in our mind.

7. There is no right way or wrong way to perform this meditation. Do what you feel is comfortable and natural for you. There is no need for stress or strain. In time you will have no need for counting "1 – 2 – 3 – 4" you will be able to close your eyes and go into a calm, relaxing and peaceful meditative state.

You can do this exercise in the morning before you start your day for 5 minutes and when you end your day for 5 minutes. Then go to 10 minutes, 15 minutes, etc. You can so do this exercise if you just experienced a stressful event. Just go to a quiet place and meditate for a few minutes to balance out your emotions.

You can also listen to this exercise by going to YouTube and typing in: **Learn a Basic Meditation: 1-2-3-4 Technique** in the search box.

THIS PAGE INTENTIONALLY LEFT BLANK

Chapter 3: Reaching Out Through Writing Letters

Why Write Letters to the Departed?

A person may ask why write letters to people who are dead? There are a two reasons to do this:

Reason 1: To make sure on your end of things that you leave nothing left unsaid to the departed. Be it good, bad, or downright ugly it's important that you get a chance to tell the departed everything you needed, wanted, and desired to tell them. To clear your mind once and for all so you can move on with your life.

Reason 2: The departed need to know everything you need to tell them – the good, the bad and the ugly so they can move on as well on their spiritual journey. Possibly make amends if people were done wrong. It is believed that as human beings we go through a "life review" once we transition and that all that we did in life is shown to us on a "movie screen" of sorts so we can see the good, bad, and ugly things we did to people and while on the "other side" we try to make things right(make amends) to help both parties move on with their respective spiritual journeys.

That's all well and good you may say but the people are dead how are they going to read them. More about that in the section called: **What to Do with The Letters After You Write Them?**

Sample Topics to Write About

Here are some sample topics to write about. Your list may be a lot different so it's important that you write about **topics that are important** to you, be they good, bad, ugly, hurtful, painful, etc., for you to express to the departed. Sample topics to write the departed about are:

1. You were a good (father, mother, etc.) because…

2. You were a bad (father, mother, etc.) because…

3. I am mad at you because…

4. You hurt me because…

5. I miss you because …

6. I love you because …

7. And whatever else you want to tell the departed…

How Long Do You Need Write These Letters For?

You write your letters to the departed until everything you need to say to them has been said. This process may that hours, days, weeks and even years. It does not need to be accomplished in one sitting. You may write a letter within a day and then another weeks later, then a month later you remember something else. A special day, holiday, event may trigger another memory about the departed that you need to express your feelings about - write another letter about the subject. Write a letter whenever something "bubbles up" from your memory that you feel needs a letter about the subject. You will get to the point that you will no longer be writing letters as everything you need to say has been said and you move on with your healing journey.

What to Do with The Letters After You Write Them?
Extreme caution is to be taken with this section as it deals with use of fire.

To perform this ceremony you will need the following items: notebook paper the type used in a 3-ring binder, a large metal empty paint can (without paint inside - available at most paint stores, hardware stores, etc.) matches or lighter (preferably a long stick matches or a long stick barbecue butane lighter) and a box of salt. The entire ceremony is to be performed outside with adult supervision if necessary.

Once the letters are written they are to be burned, one by one, until they are completely burned to ashes. It is said the burning releasing the energy attached from each letter and it is also said by burning the letters it releases the message of the letters which goes up in and with the smoke to the departed. Once the letters are burned salt is to be placed over the ashes to neutralize the energy of the letters and then then entire contents is to be discarded away from the home. A local recycling center would be preferred as the can is metal.

<u>Extreme caution is to be taken with this section as it deals with use of fire.</u>

Exercise: Write Letters to Your Departed Loved Ones
Go to your sacred space and write your letters to your departed loved one(s). While there no definite time to get started doing this task, you should start when you are moved to start writing. Then perform the ceremony of the

burning of the letters as mentioned in the previous paragraph. Make sure you do the ceremony outside, in a safe well lite and ventilated area and have fire safety in mind when conducting the letter burning ceremony.

<u>Extreme caution is to be taken with this section as it deals with use of fire.</u>

Chapter 4: Guided Imagery – A Useful Tool in Healing

What is Guided Imagery?

Guided imagery (sometimes called guided meditation, creative visualization) is a technique that focuses the mind in a proactive manner. It can be as simple as imagining oneself as managing stress in a calm manner, being more assertive in a business meeting or it can be more complex as imaging immune cells, searching, attacking, and destroying cancer cells. [1]

How Can Guided Imagery Help Me?

Guided Imagery can be helpful for an individual as to "act out", in a positive manner, in the person's mind the way they believe things should be played out in real life. In the situation of not having said goodbye before the person died, an individual can say goodbye to their loved one(s), in their mind, the individual can see, meet, and have the goodbye they did not get a chance to experience when the person was still alive. **Though Guided Imagery is not the be all and end all in experiencing closure of a loved one(s) it is another tool your healing toolbox on your healing journey.**

Exercise: Example of a Guided Imagery Exercise in Connecting with a Departed Loved One

*** This exercise is <u>not</u> to be performed while driving or performing ay type of focused activity. ***

Close your eyes and lay your hands on your lap slowly take a deep breath in through your nose and gently exhale out through your mouth.

Each time you do this I want you to relax your shoulders on every exhale so take a nice deep breath, fill your lungs with air slowly and gently breath out through your mouth again. Take a nice deep breath in slowly and gently breath out through your mouth letting the shoulders release and relax, all of the tension, all of the strain.

Again take a nice deep breathe in, fill your lungs with clean life giving oxygen.

Slowly and gently breathe out through your mouth letting the shoulders release and relax all of the tension, all of the strain. It's causing you to relax, allowing you to relax.

One last deep breathe in slowly and gently breathe out. Just bring your breathing back to normal rhythm and breathe normally.

Now imagine roots coming out from the soles of your feet. I want you to see those roots going deep, deep into the ground. As far down as you can get them to go absorbing life giving nutrients.

Now I want to you to see yourself surrounded by a pure white light. Feel this light, this energy as it forms around you like a cloak of pure protection.

Do your best to see it. Do your best to feel it. There is no right or wrong way. Just do what feels right to you.

Sense this light, this energy as it enters your body and fills you with pure love.

This light comes from the source of everything.

This light brings with it peace and relaxation.

You are a part of that energy, and that energy is part of you.

You start to relax even more.

I'm going to count up to the number three and with each number I count take a nice deep breath and gently release and relax.

One, take a nice deep breath and release and relax.

Two, take a nice deep breath and release and relax.

Three, take a nice deep breath and release and relax.

Now just release and relax and breath normally.

Now this time, every time you exhale, I want you to say **in your mind** the word RELAX, so deeply breath in, slowly and gently breath out the word RELAX.

One more time breathe in slowly and gently breath out saying the word RELAX.

Now just let your breathing come back to its normal.
Just release and relax all of the tension from your body.
You are at peace; you are very relaxed.
In your mind, I want you to go to a private island. Your private beautiful island.

I want you to see it surrounded by the deepest blue ocean you have ever seen.

Watch it as it takes shape all around you and you can hear the waves gently lapping on the shore and you can smell that wonderful smell of the sea.

You are on your beach with sand beneath your bare feet.

Feel the sand beneath your toes.

Feel it. Let all of your senses come alive!

You turn and look at the sea, the deepest blue sea you have ever seen.

The sun is shining down creating sparkles in the water.

It fills your heart with joy to look at it and you feel at home here because this is your private place, your private beautiful sanctuary.

The place where you are always safe and relaxed.

The place where you feel truly at home.

Now always remember you are safe and protected here.

You are loved and you are protected always.

You walk back along your beach back towards a magical forest and you can see the well-worn paths that you have walked many times before.

There are flowers all around you.

Beautiful flowers with colors that are indescribable!

It's like the colors are alive with life themselves.

You see butterflies floating in the air as they dance past you.

The birds are high in the sky flying from branch to branch see them full of joy and happiness.

The sun is shining down upon you making you feel warm and comfortable.

And there is a gentle breeze upon your skin as you walk.

Ahead of you see an old high wall with a wooden door in the center of it.

You walked up to the door and gently push it open as you step through the door and come out the other side and you find yourself in a field.

Field of beautiful flowers, they are everywhere.

The smell of the flowers is intoxicating, and you start to feel the beginning of a memory.

You start to remember a loved one in Spirit.

You are remembering someone special in your life.

Someone who now lives in the spirit world.

You start to walk across the field and among the wonderful flowers.

You can still hear the birds in the distance.

You stop for a moment and just enjoy being there.

You are surrounded by fields of flowers swaying in the gentle breeze.

And you feel at so peaceful and so at home.

You are so relaxed!

As you walk further still, you see ahead of you just at the end of the field the shape of the person starting to form.

You realize that the person is walking towards you.

As they draw closer to you, you recognize the person.

You can now see that it is the very special person you know and love.

The person who now lives in the spirit world.

The person who is now in front of YOU.

Your heart swells with joy and love for this person.

You can see their smile, their beautiful face, the wonderful warm eyes as they raise their arms to hold you tight.

The love you feel for them is very strong and powerful.

You are so happy and filled full of love and to see this person again.

This person whom you love with all your heart.

I want you to spend some time with your loved one and just to enjoy being with them as you both spend time in the field of flowers together.

Take time to chat. In your mind, ask the person things you want to know.

Tell them how much you miss them.

They are never ever far away from you.

Always helping you, guiding you and loving you.

You take their arm as you begin your walk together.

LONG PAUSE HERE

In a few moments it will be time to part company.

Now it's time to let your loved one return to the spirit world.

It is time for them to go back home where they will wait for you until it is your time to join them, and you can be together again, but that time is <u>NOT</u> now.

They embrace you once more and smile, a beautiful smile they are always had.

And you feel eternally grateful that you had this time with them once more.

But you know that at any time you can always come back to this special place and be with them once again.

Anytime you want to come back to this place, you can.
You turn now and walk back the way you came.
As you now turn back walking through the fields of flowers back to the wooden door and the old wall.

And your heart is filled with joy and peace and love.

You now know that life is really wonderful, despite all of its ups and downs.

You step back through the door back to your own special place your own private beautiful island.

And you walk back along the well-trodden path.

Down to your beach.

And you can see the ocean again.

You take one last look around this beautiful place of yours the place where you are peace.

And you feel a peace that you have never felt before.

You now know that your loved ones are never far away.

And then you can visit them anytime you want.

Now it's time for you to bring your consciousness back to the here and now.

Back into the room bringing to all the love joy and peace back with you.

And you will carry it in your heart always.

So take a nice deep breathe in and slowly and breathe out.

Again nice deep breathe in and slowly and gently breathe out.

One last breathe in and slowly and gently breathe out.

Now gently wiggle your fingers and your toes and whenever you are ready, slowly, and gently.

Slow open your eyes!

Coming back to the here and now. Feeling totally refreshed, reenergize, and revitalized.

Remembering everything you just experienced.

*** This exercise is <u>not</u> to be performed while driving or performing any type of focused activity. ***

Chapter 5: Mediumship – Fact or Fiction

What is a Medium and Mediumship?

The term Medium refers to a person with a psychic ability to communicate with a spiritual entity. Mediumship involves cooperative communication between a human and one or more discarnate, spirit personalities. [2]

Why Work with a Medium?

Working with a Medium is yet another tool in your healing toolbox. Mediums use their skills (as previous mentioned) to help people communicate with the deceased loved one(s). Most Mediums are very supportive, caring and understanding individuals that will assist you on your healing journey. As you have been reading, you'll noticed there are various tools to assist you on your journey. You may choose to use all of them, some of them, none of them or you may create your own. Only you know what is right for you and what tools you are comfortable using for your healing journey.

Should I Work with a Medium?

Working with a Medium is a very personal decision that only you can make for yourself. It is advisable to do your homework/research on Mediumship as there are many sources online where you can read, see, and hear about Mediumship. It is also advisable to speak to as many people as you can about their experiences in working with a Medium. Keep in mind as with all services some people will have positive experiences and some people will have not so good experiences. Personally, I use the "Rule of 3" if I work with 3 separate and different people for a given service (e.g. Chiropractor, Acupuncturist, etc.) and I have negative experiences with all three then its pretty clear to me that particular service is not right for me. Conversely, if work with 3 separate and different people for a given service and the first experience was bad and the next two experiences were good, then it tells me it's not the service that was not a good fit but rather the person delivering that service that was not a good fit for me. To recap, do your your due diligence before you make your decision about using this service. Mediumship has and continues to help and heal many people on their bereavement healing journey and this yet another tool in your healing toolbox.

Mediumship and Religion

In many religions, especially in Catholicism, Mediumship is not to be used and is to be kept away from people as something that is that is no good, wrong, and downright bad. Each religion has their reasons as to why Mediumship is wrong or bad, whether their reasons are valid remains to be seen. I'm sure, like everything in else in life some people had bad experiences with Mediumship, some people were hurt by it and misinterpreted what the Medium and the messages were really trying to say to the listeners. Though I am an Inter-Faith (All-Faiths) Minister, and understand, appreciate, and even practice various spiritual traditions, I still am a Catholic to a larger extent. Though I neither currently embrace nor deny my Catholic faith (the church run by man versus the teachings which I hold to be true) I was raised in that tradition, and I respect the teachings of my faith. It is for the reasons I have just mentioned that I have written the discussion below and ultimately it is your decision whether Mediumship is right for you and is to be used in your healing journey and one of your tools in your "healing toolbox".

The Use of Mediums:

Point and Counter-Point Opinion then <u>You</u> Decide

<u>**Point**</u>**:** Though I am an Inter-Faith (All-Faiths) Minister (**www.GodLovesYouAndMe.org**) I was raised in the Catholic tradition and part of the Catholic tradition is the belief in sacred text - The Holy Bible. In The Holy Bible there are many verses that state and suggest that people <u>should not</u> consult (work with) Mediums and like people. One verse of The Holy Bible in the New Living Translation (NLT) Bible states that: "For false messiahs and false prophets will rise up and perform great signs and wonders so as to deceive, if possible, even God's chosen ones." Matthew 24:24 NLT (New Living Translation Bible). I choose the New Living Translation Bible as it is more easily understandable for the modern day age. There are other passages from The Holy Bible that state a similar message and in much stronger terms to avoid Mediums.

Count-Point: As I previously stated, being an Inter-Faith Minister and having been raised in the Catholic tradition and believing in a loving God I am hard pressed to believe that God would want his/her children to suffer open emotional wounds of not receiving closure with loved ones that have passed away. The Medium provides a valuable service that no one else can provide unless they have that particular skill and ability. The Medium's insights which are delivered as a reading to the individual and/or individuals, which many times becomes a healing to the person to get closure on open emotional issues between the two parties, the departed and the living. Many people go to their graves with open emotional issues never resolved between loved ones. Is this what a loving God desires in the lives of his/her children to have them suffer emotional wounds their entire lives? I say no, that is why, I believe, God has created people that have such an ability and skill.

Most Mediums are very caring, compassionate, and helping individuals as to help other people achieve better lives with their readings and healings.

I have personally worked with Mediums that have helped me get closure with loved ones. Most of my experiences in working with Mediums has been positive some were not that good but were not terrible. As with all services some people are better than others in delivering the services they provide.

You Decide: As with all decisions to be made in life ultimately **YOU** are the one making them and live with the outcome of those decisions, be it good or not so good. You must understand the impact of going to see and work with a Medium. And the impact of working with a Medium if you choose to tell others; family members, loved ones, friends, the world, etc. Later in this chapter I will offer some suggested guidance on what to be aware of when looking to work with a Medium that may assist you on your journey. Once again, the decision is ultimately yours to make.

What to Look For When Working with a Medium

As with any time you are seeking to hire a person delivering services to you, I would be doing the follow:

1. Check on-line reviews for the individual. Read the NEGATIVE ones first then read the Positive reviews. By reading the negatives reviews you can get a real understanding about the person working relationship with others. The comments tend to be real, valid and give a true picture of the service delivered or tend to be people that like to complain. For example, "The service they delivered was okay, but the way they were dressed was terrible.

I was so embarrassed for them". Clearly that review as NOTHING to say that tells me the quality of the service that the person provided.

2. Ask for References. Most people that have been in business for a while should be able to provide you with people they have worked with in the past and will provide a reference for the services they delivered. Call the references and get some feedback on their experience with the Medium.

3. See the Medium LIVE! Go to an event where the Medium is delivering a sample of their services. See the Medium "in action – live" so you can get a feeling if it feels right to work with this individual, especially with such a personal matter as the loss of a loved one(s).

Example of a Working Medium – Elizabeth Rose

An example of having a Mediumship session with Elizabeth Rose would consist of making a telephone appointment for a 30, 60 or 90 minute session. Many people have heard of *The Long Island Medium*. Elizabeth Rose channels messages from deceased loved ones. In contrast, Elizabeth is more like the medium played by *Whoopi Goldberg* in the movie, "*Ghost*" but she a **Clear Channel** (Deep Trance Channel) of divine guidance from God, Christ, Seraphim (High Order of Angels), Archangels, Angels, Ascended Masters, and sometimes deceased loved ones. All "step-in" and move her body in different ways in order to heal, transmit healing energies and speak through her.

Elizabeth Rose has facilitated individuals and groups in thousands of hours of Trance Channeling, Energy Healing, Channeled Hypnosis, Channeled Yoga, Dream Interpretation plus many other protocols. She left a 25-year institutional investment career to be a hypnotist which led to deep trance channeling, writing, plus teaching hypnosis and healing certification courses and workshops. Today she teaches, channels messages and healing for clients around the globe. Elizabeth is an expert in consciousness exploration using channeling, hypnosis, spiritual healing, and a range of other powerful modalities: Author, Public Speaker, NGH Certified Hypnosis Instructor, Certified Healing Arts Facilitator, Channeled Yoga Instructor, Deep Trance Channel

She can be reached **www.TheRoseCottage.ca** in Saint John, New Brunswick, Canada and works with clients via SKYPE, ZOOM or by Telephone.

Exercise: Prepare Questions for Your Reading with a Medium

Before working and going to meet with a Medium, with a clear mind, write approximately a dozen questions you would like to ask, in order of the priority that you need them answered. Keep in mind that session may be any where from 30 minutes to 120 minutes depending how the Medium run their practice, their availability, their fees etc. With that said it is high unlikely that all of your questions will be answered the first session and that if you want all of your questions answered you will require multiple sessions with the Medium. Furthermore, be advised that your first question may lead to an answer that you may lead you to another question based on the answer you just received.

Ask the Medium you will be working with if they and/or you can record the session as you may be experiencing an array of different emotions during your session and listening to the session when you are alone, calm, cool and collected may yield things that you did not hear or understand properly at the time of the reading with the Medium.

THIS

PAGE

INTENTIONALLY

LEFT

BLANK

Chapter 6: Connecting with Nature

Why Nature is So Important?

So why is nature so important to our existence as human beings? Besides the basic elements of life: water, air, earth and fire, nature provides all of us with life giving sustenance, from the food that we eat to the houses in which we live in, nature is a part of all of us, directly and indirectly.

Nature provides our being with renewal on all levels of our being – physically, mentally, emotionally, and spiritually. On the physical level with the food that we eat, mentally it shows us that everything has a place and a purpose, and it lives it purpose in each movement, emotionally there is love from nature (Mother Earth) as it provides for all of our needs and spiritually, as one quiets their mind you will see, know and understand that we are all connected and we all need each other in good times and in not so good times. You will find in nature peace and solace that cannot be found in no other place that is manmade. The connection with nature is a sacred one and is worthy of taking the time to build and grow that connection as you will be a better person for it and be another tool in your healing and your healing toolbox.

Nature Your Sacred Space

You can also choose nature as an additional sacred space. Once you start enjoying being in nature, being one with nature and seeing the beauty of nature this will lead a certain calm, peace and serenity coming upon you. It will help you to put things in a better perspective. There will come a time of understanding that while we are all here for a reason and purpose, then there comes a time when it is time to go back to where we came from. Sometimes that happens in a logical, structured, and calm manner and sometimes it happens in just the opposite manner for reasons unknown to us all. There are times we are not meant to know those reasons and may be there comes a time we will be told those reasons in another place and another time.

Nature is always there for all of us, not judging us and accepting us for who we are just as we are. The rock in nature does not pretend to be a tree as the tree does not pretend to be the rock. Each has it own purpose and reason for being. Neither claims to be anything other then themselves for all to see. View nature as a place to be yourself with no one or no thing judging you and making you think you are anything less than the ultimate creation of GOD.

Nature Helps You Get Closer to God

Once you start spending time in nature with all it's awe inspiring majesty, scenery, and calming effect you will start noticing, appreciating, and understanding that all of this cannot be here by accident and that there must be some higher power orchestrating all of this nature from happening. How do the flowers know when and how to blossom? How do the fish know how to swim? How do the birds know how to migrate south in the winter? The list is endless. There must be something creating, controlling and making this all happen. I believe it to be GOD, the Creator of all things. If GOD cares so much about the loneliest piece of grass, imagine how GOD cares about humankind, GOD's beloved children.

Nature is a perfect place to pray and mediate on GOD and your current circumstance of having lost a loved one(s).

It is also a very good place to build your relationship with GOD even if you never had one before. If you do have a relationship with GOD it's a good place to make it stronger. A major milestone in my life is having felt GOD's love. It was a feeling pure, unconditional, and nonjudgmental love. How no words were exchanged just love was sent to me. That experience and moment in time still moves me to this day. Even these words do not do the experience justice. I do urge you to build your relationship with GOD and GOD will help you manage your pain of having lost a loved one(s) in such a sudden, shocking, and devastating manner.

Exercise: Spend Time in Nature

The exercise here is a simple one, find some nature in your area of the world, be it a backyard, a park or whatever is close at hand and do the exercises in this book. Spend some time journaling, praying, meditating and just spend some time "unplugging your mind" and recharging your batteries – physically, mentally, emotionally, and spiritually. It will do you a world of good. It will give you the strength to continue your healing journey of having lost your loved one(s) and give you the courage to carry on in life.

Chapter 7: GOD Told Me to Tell You You're Not Alone

Why Go to GOD?

Whether you believe in GOD as the ultimate Creator of all things or not, or your mad at GOD for taking away your loved ones with no warning or you just don't believe in a high being period, it's good to know that such a being does indeed exist for the better meant of humankind. Everyone tends to have or have not there own relationship with GOD and it is not the purpose of this book to debate whether or not GOD does truly exist. The main message here is that a relationship with GOD is possible at anytime in your life, whether you never had a relationship with GOD, the presence of GOD is always available to all humankind at anytime and under any circumstances. And it's okay to be mad at GOD as GOD can handle it and is always there for all of us and is always forgiving. Imagine GOD as all loving being that does not judge us and accepts all of us just as we are with unconditional love. GOD is always there for you, your departed loved and all the people in your life. GOD is love and GOD sends YOU love.

The Power of Prayer

What is prayer and why should you pray? While there are various technical definitions what prayer is, in short prayer is communication with GOD, Source or whatever you believe GOD is to you. It is a good practice to use prayer and mediation with each other as it said, "If a person wants to **speak** with GOD they **pray** and if a person wants to **hear** GOD they **meditate**."

Like meditation there is no right way or wrong way to pray. Similar to meditation, a person may use a standard process like written prayers when praying and guided meditation when meditating or create and/or just pray directly from your heart. GOD will always understand the intention of your prayers. The important thing is that you pray as often as you see fit for comfort, grace, and guidance while you are going through your healing journey and beyond.

Regarding why should you pray? It gives a person a feeling of comfort knowing that you are not alone, not going through your healing journey alone and that there is a BEING there in your life always willing to listen to you in good times and in bad.

That's what GOD told me to tell you, that you're not alone and that you will be comforted in your time of need. Though the comfort may not come at the exact moment when you what it to come and may not be in the form of comfort that you expect it to come, GOD will never fail you in your time of need. Rest if your must don't you quit. GOD also told me to tell you – GOD sends you love!

Sample Prayers for the Departed

Below are some sample prayers for the departed souls in your life.

Prayers for the Dead [3]

Prayer for the Soul to Rest in Peace

We thank You GOD for the passing of our brother/sister. We exalt Your name for the good life he/she lived. We pray oh Lord, that everlasting life be given unto him or her. And as he or she abides in Your garden, let Your angels touch what he/she cannot touch again. GOD, be with his/her soul and may he/she rest in perfect eternal peace. Amen

Short Prayer for the Dead

Eternal rest grant unto him/her, O Lord, and let perpetual light shine upon him/her. May he rest in peace. Love always. Amen

Prayer for Grieving

Lord God above, we, Your humble children kneel before you today in reverence. We know You're the greatest and You're the king of all kings. So, we pray You uplift our heart and soul so that we may cast away our sorrows oh Lord. Give us the strength to surpass this situation. No one dies without Your say-so and thus, we rejoice over this triumph, and we pray You be with our deceased brother/sister. We thank you for the answered prayer, Amen.

Prayer for Death of a Loved One

May the light of Jesus and the Angels bring Peace and Salvation to my _____. May he/she rest in peace knowing that his soul belongs to GOD and GOD only. All is well with us _____ go home and rest. We love you and one day soon we will see you in HEAVEN! Amen.

Prayer for a Departed Soul

Heavenly GOD bless ____ and have mercy on his eternal soul; forgive his/her trespasses; grant him/her peace for he/she was a faithful man/woman who loved his fellow humans; bless his/her departed soul and welcome him/her into the joy of everlasting brightness in heaven, Amen.

Prayer for Wife/Mother/Grandmother Who Passed

I commend you, my dear wife, mother, and grandmother to Almighty GOD, and entrust you to your creator. May you rest in the arms of the Lord who formed you from the dust of the earth.

Please watch over our family in these difficult times. May Holy Mary, the angels and all the saints welcome you now that you have gone forth from this life. Amen.

Prayer for the Soul of a Mother/Father

Dear GOD, I thank You for taking care of my father/mother during their life on Earth. I thank You for giving them the opportunity to bring me into this world and I likewise thank You for the opportunity to have this prayer. I rejoice over the life that he/she led while alive and for the good deeds he/she accomplished. Lord GOD, I thusly pray for the soul of my deceased mother/father and that You take care of him/her on his/her way to Your holy Kingdom. I thank you for listening to my prayers oh Lord, Amen.

Prayer for a Brother/Sister

As far as I remember, my brother/sister has been with me through all the ups and downs of life. We ate and played together, gave advice to each other, and kept no secret from one another. Now, seeing as he/she is gone, I pray that he/she finds everlasting life and eternal happiness in Your powerful embrace. I pray You watch over his/her wife/husband/children/investments on Earth and let Your gaze shift not oh Lord. I thank You for this prayer session, I pray. Amen.

Exercise: Prayer and Meditation

While there is no prescribed method and time a person should pray and meditate it is just good "spiritual hygiene". And like all hygiene it is a good practice to do it daily or as often as possible. You can pray and mediate in your sacred space, in nature, in a religious building of your choosing regardless of the place, time and location (other than driving) it is just a good practice to get into to help grant you peace and calm in your day. If you should miss a day or so just pick up your prayer and meditation practice wear you left it and continue with it once again you will feel so much better that you did.

THIS PAGE INTENTIONALLY LEFT BLANK

Conclusion

Losing a loved one(s) is never easy especially if the loved one(s) was taken suddenly without warning and without having the ability to say goodbye. As mentioned previously, the tools, techniques and methods in this book are to be used **"in addition to and not instead of"** the methods, traditions, and therapies that the reader is comfortable using.

Let's briefly recap the tools discussed in this book:

In **Chapter 1: YOU are Important** there was a discussion of the importance of taking care of yourself through your healing journey and adding tools to your "healing toolbox" like creating sacred space for yourself and starting the process of journaling.

Chapter 2: Meditation: Centering Yourself in Mind, Body and Spirit demonstrates how essential meditation is to your wellbeing – physically, mentally, emotionally, and spiritually and how using the 1-2-3-4 method of meditation will help you and can be done anytime and anyplace (though not while driving) to restore you back to your center and calmness.

In **Chapter 3: Reaching Out Through Writing Letters** is a very good technique to say all the things that needed to be said to your departed loved one(s) that were not said and the ceremony to ensure they receive your messages.

Chapter 4 - Guided Imagery: A Useful Tool in Healing you now have another tool to help get closure between you and your loved one(s). A sample exercise is provided in the chapter.

In **Chapter 5 - Mediumship: Fact or Fiction** you will learn about the tool of Mediumship and working with a Medium and if this is a good tool for you on your healing journey. How to find a Medium and what things you should look for in working with a Medium and much more.

Chapter 6: Connecting with Nature learn the importance of connecting, being and of sitting in nature to help you recharge your yourself and to use some if not all of the tools that you have learned about in this book while being in nature.

In **Chapter 7: GOD Told Me to Tell You You're Not Alone.** Learn that GOD is there for you always, the Power of Prayer and read Prayers for the Departed.

It has been the hope of this book to give the reader additional tools for the bereavement process and provide additional tools for the reader's "healing toolbox" to help make the healing journey smoother, more compassionate and loving one.

Remember that you do not walk alone in your healing journey as there are many seen and unseen that are with you and helping to comfort you along the way.

Remember GOD is always with you

and

GOD sends you love!

Footnotes

[1] **What is Guide Imagery?**

https://www.healthjourneys.com/guided-imagery-101

[2] **What is a Medium and Mediumship?**

https://www.newworldencyclopedia.org/entry/Mediumship

[3] **Prayers for the Dead**

https://www.holylandprayer.com/prayer_for/prayers-for-the-dead/

THIS PAGE INTENTIONALLY LEFT BLANK

Bibliography

DAversa, Oreste J. **Write Your Own Funeral Service.** Paramus, NJ. Cutting Edge Technology Publishing. 2021.

DAversa, Oreste J. **Life Beyond the Pandemic: A New Journey Handbook.** Paramus, NJ. Cutting Edge Technology Publishing. 2021.

Noel, Brook and Blair, Pamela D. **I Wasn't Ready to Say Goodbye**. Naperville, Ill. Sourcebooks, Inc. 2000

THIS PAGE INTENTIONALLY LEFT BLANK

Grief Resources

The website Grief Speaks (**http://www.griefspeaks.com/**) has tremendous amounts of resources some are posted below:

National Support Groups

Alcoholics Anonymous: www.AA.org (locate a meeting or find information about alcoholism, find groups for teens, family and friends affected by alcohol.

ACCESS (Aircraft Casualty Emotional Support Services)
This is a national network for those who have lost a loved one in an aircraft-related tragedy. It matches the bereaved person with volunteers who have previously experienced a similar loss. It is only email or phone support. **www.accesshelp.org**

American Association of Retired Persons (AARP)
Online bereavement support   **www.aarp.org**

American Association of Suicidology
This national organization offers resources for suicide prevention and survivors of suicide (SOS). They provide a newsletter, a directory of resources for suicide prevention, conferences, and referrals to local SOS chapters. **www.suicidology.org**

American Foundation for Suicide Prevention (AFSP): www.afsp.org information for survivors and a 24/7 National Lifeline: 1-800-273-TALK (8255)

Autoerotic Asphyxiation Support: Online organization provides a supportive message board for family and friends of those who have died by autoerotic asphyxiation.
www.groups.yahoo.com/group/autoeroticasphyxiationsupport

Center for Adoption Support: National center for adoption support, webinars, newsletters, forums. **www.adoptionsupport.org**

Coalition to Support Grieving Students: Support, articles, and resources to help students, educators and parents support grieving students. www.grievingstudents.org

The Compassionate Friends: (TCF) This is the largest self-help organization in the world for bereaved parents, siblings and grandparents. They provide more than 650 local chapters in the United States and Canada, with national and regional conferences. TCF offers national and local newsletters, books and tapes and other related bereavement resources. **www.compassionatefriends.org**

COPS (Concerns of Police Survivors, Inc.) This national organization provides resources for the surviving families of law enforcement officers killed in the line of duty. They sponsor the National Police Survivors' Conference each May, special hands on programs for survivors, a summer camp for children (ages 6-14) and their parent/guardian, parents' retreats, spousal retreats. Outward Bound experiences for young adults (15-20) a sibling retreat and an adult children's and in-laws retreat.www.nationalcops.org Resources for the surviving families of law enforcement officers killed in the line of duty. **www.nationalcops.org**

Delta Society: Online organization maintains a list of pet bereavement support groups, pet loss resource persons, counselors and hotlines. **www.deltasociety.org**

Grief Recovery After A Substance Passing: was created to help provide sources of help, compassion and most of all understanding, for families or individuals who have had a loved one die as a result of substance abuse or addiction. **www.grasphelp.org** 760-262-8612

Grief Share: National organization is a network of Christian support groups for the bereaved. **www.griefshare.org**

GRIEF SPEAKS: resource for information about grieving children, teens and adults. Books lists, links, and specific loss information. **www.griefspeaks.com**

GROWW (Grief Recovery Online (founded by) Widows and Widowers: bereavement chat rooms dealing with specific losses (child, spouse, parent, sudden death, long term illness, gay and lesbian, men etc.) **www.groww.org**

Hospice Net: helps teens with grief due to life threatening illnesses **www.hospicenet.org**

Treatment for Mesothelioma Learn all there is to know about Mesothelioma and the treatments available. From surgery to chemotherapy, emerging treatments, and even alternative therapies, patients have options. With loved ones, with all the information, and with a great medical team, you can make the right choices about your mesothelioma treatment. Click on the above link to find out more or visit **www.mesothelioma.net**

Mesothelioma Veterans Center: This organization reaches veterans and their families who have been affected by mesothelioma and connect them to their website, which offers free veteran specific resources and support. 1/3 of all cases of this disease affect veterans. Since 2004 over 5000 veterans have died from mesothelioma The website is: **www.mesotheliomaVeterans.org**

Mesothelioma Lawyer Center: Offer comprehensive asbestos and mesothelioma information, with an emphasis on the legal options available to asbestos victims. Check out their website at: **www.MesotheliomaLawyerCenter.org/mesothelioma-lawyer/**

The Mesothelioma Group: published a very informative guide to understanding
cancer: **http://www.mesotheliomagroup.com/understanding-cancer/**

Mothers Against Drunk Drivers (MADD): A National organization dedicated to stopping drunk driving and to supporting victims of this violent crime.
www.madd.org   Call: 1-800-GET-MADD

Mothers in Sympathy and Support (MISS): organization dedicated to supporting parents one to one after the death of an infant or young child.
www.missfoundation.org   Call 1-623-979-1000

National Alliance for the Mentally Ill: Family support and self-help groups. **www.nami.org**   1-800-950-NAMI

National Fallen Firefighters Foundation Survivors Support Network: National organization provides emotional support to spouses, families, and friends who have died in the line of duty. Members are matched with survivors of similar experience to help them cope. **www.firehero.org**

National Hospice and Palliative Care Organization (NHPCO): referrals to more than 2100 hospices, a national newsletter, magazine, and professional conferences.
www.nhpco.org

National Institute of Mental Health: Information on depression and other mental illnesses **www.nimh.nih.gov** 1-800-421-4211

National Mental Illness Screening Project: locate a free, confidential screening site near you.
 www.nmisp.org   1-800-573-4433

National Students of Ailing Mothers and Fathers Support Network (AMF): A network of university students helping each other cope with the serious illness or death of a parent or loved one. Developing campus based mutual support groups around the US and offer an online newsletter, online chats and service projects. Website provides information, group development guidelines, and a list of universities currently developing support groups.
www.studentsofamf.org

1 in 6: Providing Courage, Hope and Strength to men who have had unwanted or abusive sexual experiences in childhood. Help them to live healthier and happier lives. Provides resources for men and those who care about them. **www.1in6.org**

Parents of Murdered Children: (POMC): largest self-help organization in the world for parents, families, friends and other victims of homicide. POMC has more than 400 local chapters and contact persons in the US and abroad. In addition to groups, they provide newsletters and offer conferences.
www.pomc.org   1-513-721-5683

Rainbows: International organization offering peer support groups in churches, schools or social agencies for children and adults who are grieving a death, divorce or other painful transition in their family. **www.rainbows.org** 1-847-952-1774

RAINN: Rape, Abuse, and Incest National Network: The nation's largest anti-sexual violence organization. National Sexual Assault Hot line: 1-800-656-HOPE. call 24/7. Website provides help, resources, information, and links. **www.RAINN.org**

SIDS Alliance: National organization supporting families who have suffered sudden infant death syndrome. SIDS Alliance has more than 50 local chapters and offers a newsletter and conferences.
www.firstcandle.org   1-800-221-SIDS

Society for the Prevention of Teen Suicide: Great resource for teens, educators and parents. Short film, Not My Kid, educators can receive CEU's and a lot of information about depression and helping a friend. Provides the 24/7 National Lifeline: 1-800-273-TALK (8255) **www.sptsnj.org**

TAPS (Tragedy Assistance Program for Survivors): National network providing support for persons who have lost a loved one serving in the armed forces (Army, Air Force, Navy, Marine Corps, National Guard, Reserves, Service Academies, Coast Guard, and contractors serving beside the military). TAPS offers crisis information, problem solving assistance and liaison with military agencies. Also provides extensive youth programs and an annual multigenerational gathering in Washington DC. **www.taps.org** 1-800-959-8277

The Trevor Project: A 24/7 suicide prevention hotline for LGBTQ youth. They also run a Dear Trevor Project that allows GLBTQ youth to ask questions via the Internet. **www.thetrevorproject.org** 1-866-488-7386 (866-4-U-Trevor)

Twin-less Twin Support Group: International support network that provides mutual support for twins and other multiples who have lost their twin or multiple. **www.twinlesstwins.org** 1-888-205-8962

Wings of Light, Inc. National Organization provides support and information to individuals affected by aviation accidents. Provides separate networks for airplane accident survivors, family and friends of persons killed in airplane accidents, and person involved in rescue, recovery and investigation of crashes.
www.wingsoflight.org 1-623-516-1115

Wounded Warrior Project: Organization that provides support, information and resources to wounded warriors and their families. **Restore** is an online, multi-media tool that offers warriors and caregivers the chance to learn about readjustment challenges. Warriors can take self-assessments and participate in interactive skill-building exercises that provide practical ways to deal with combat and operational stress. Restore is an anonymous environment that is only accessible through WWP Connect, our social network for WWP alumni, caregivers and staff. **www.woundedwarriorproject.org** 1-877-TEAM-WWP **(904-296-7350)**

Looking for Referrals:

American Psychiatric Association: Information and referrals to psychiatrists in your area, **www.psych.org** 1-888-852-8330

American Psychological Association: information and referrals to psychologists in your area,
www.apa.org helping.apa.org 1-800-964-2000

National Association of Social Workers: information and referrals to social workers in your area:
www.socialworker.org 1-800-638-8799

Bereaved Parents of the USA: This national support group for bereaved parents, siblings and grandparents offers a newsletter, referrals to local chapters and conferences.
www.bereavedparents.org

Center for Suicide Prevention: SIEC has extensive info on suicide prevention, postvention, and intervention efforts and trends. They offer a newsletter and referrals to local support services.
www.suicideinfo.ca

Children of September 11th: Support, information, and referrals for families: **www.childrenofseptember11.org**

American Childhood Cancer Society: helps children battle and overcome cancer: **http://www.acco.org**

Delta Society: National organization maintains a list of pet bereavement support groups, pet loss persons, counselors, and hotlines. **www.deltasociety.org**

Grief Share: This national organization with 3200 affiliated groups is a network of Christian support groups for the bereaved. It provides info and referrals, literature and help in starting groups. **www.griefshare.org**

Mothers Against Drunk Drivers (MADD): National organization dedicated to stopping drunk driving and to supporting victims of this violent crime. MADD has over 300 local chapters and offers victim support groups for the bereaved. There is a newsletter, magazine, training programs and conferences. Phone: 800-GET-MADD **www.madd.org**

Mothers in Sympathy and Support (MISS): MISS is an organization dedicated to supporting parents' one-to-one after the death of an infant or young child.**www.missfoundation.org**

National Alliance for Grieving Children
http://nationalallianceforgrievingchildren.org

National Fallen Firefighters Foundation Survivors Support Network: National organization provides emotional support to spouses, families, and friends of firefighters who have died in the line of duty. Members are matched with survivors of similar experiences to help them cope during the difficult months following the death. **www.firehero.org**

National Hospice and Palliative Care Organization (NHPCO): Referrals to over 2100 hospices, a national newsletter, magazine, volunteer and professional conferences, and related support services. **www.nhpco.org**

National Students of Ailing Mothers and Fathers Support Network (AMF): AMF is a network of university students helping each other cope with the serious illness or death of a parent or loved one. They are actively developing campus-based mutual support groups around the US and also offer an online newsletter, online chats, and service projects. Their web site provides information, group development guidelines, and a listing of universities currently developing support groups. **www.studentsofamf.org**

Parents of Murdered Children (POMC): Largest self-help organization in the world for parents, families, friends, and other victims of homicide. POMC has more than 400 local chapters and contact persons in the US and abroad. They have groups, newsletters and offer conferences. # 513-721-5683 **www.pomc.org**

Pet Loss Grief Support Website: Moderated board offers support and understanding for persons grieving the loss of their pet or who have a pet this is ill. It also offers Monday Pet Loss Candle Ceremony, a chat room, tribute pages and other resources. **www.petloss.com**

RAINBOWS: International organization with 8600 groups, offering peer support groups in churches, schools, or social agencies for children and adults who are grieving a death, divorce or other painful transition in the family. 800-266-3206 **www.rainbows.org**

SIDS Alliance: National organization supporting families who have suffered sudden infant death syndrome. SIDS Alliance has more than 50 local chapters and offers a newsletter and conferences. 800-221-SIDS **www.firstcandle.org**

TAPS (Tragedy Assistance Program for Survivors): National network providing support for persons who have lost a loved one while serving in the armed forces (Army, Air Force, Navy, Marine Corps, National Guard, Reserves, Service Academies, Coast Guard, and contractors serving beside military). Offers networking, crisis info, problem solving assistance and liaison with military agencies. There are also extensive TAPS youth programs and an annual multi-generational gathering in Wash DC. 800-959-8277 **www.taps.org**

Twinless Twin Support Group: This is an international support network that provides mutual support for twins and other multiples who have lost their twin or multiple(s).
888-205-8962   email: contact@twinlesstwins.org
www.twinlesstwins.org

Wings of Light: National organization provides support and information to individuals affected by aviation accidents. Provides separate networks for airplane accident survivors, families and friends of persons killed in airplane accidents and persons involved in rescue, recovery and investigation of crashes. 623-516-1115
www.wingsoflight.org

NOTES

NOTES

Part Two (Book):

Write Your Own Funeral Service

Prepare and Deliver Your Own
Funeral Service/Celebration of Life for
Family Members, Friends and Loved Ones That Were Not
Able to Receive a Proper Burial Service

© Copyright www.GodLovesYouAndMe.org

Rev. Oreste J. D'Aversa

PUBLISHER'S NOTE

This book is designed to provide accurate and authoritative. Information in regard to the subject matter covered. It is sold with the understanding that neither the author nor publisher is engaged in rendering psychological, legal, or other professional service. If psychological, legal, professional advice or other expert assistance is required, the services of a professional, in that field should be sought. The principles and concepts presented in this book are the opinions of the author and based on his interpretations of the aforementioned principles. Neither the author nor publisher is liable or responsible to any person or entity for any errors contained on this book, website, or for any special, incidental, or consequential damage caused or alleged to be caused directly or indirectly by the information contained on this book or website. Any application of the techniques, ideas and suggestions in this book is at the reader's sole discretion and risk.

Copyright © Oreste J. D'Aversa, 2021. All rights reserved.

No part of this publication may be reproduced, redistributed, taught, stored in a retrieval system, or transmitted, in any form, or by any means, electronic, mechanical, photocopy, recording, or otherwise, without the prior written permission of the publisher.

FIRST EDITION

ISBN: 978-1-952294-12-9

Library of Congress Control Number: 2021915355

Published by: Cutting Edge Technology Publishing

The Picture on the Cover – The Phoenix

The Phoenix bird symbolizes immortality, resurrection, and life after death, and in ancient Greek and Egyptian mythology, it is associated with the sun god.

Associated with the sun, a phoenix obtains new life by arising from the ashes of its predecessor. Some legends say it dies in a show of flames and combustion, others that it simply dies and decomposes before being born again.

NOTES

Dedication

This book is dedicated to all people who have lost loved ones in their lives without having a chance to say goodbye in a proper, respectful, and loving manner. May your burden be lightened a little and may you find comfort in knowing that the people you love are in a better place and that they send you love in return.

NOTES

Table of Contents

1 About the Author 115

2. Introduction 117

3. Memorial Service 121

4. Funeral Prayers/Quotes 163

5. Conclusion 215

6. Worksheets 219

7. Footnotes 261

8. Bibliography 267

NOTES

1. About the Author

Rev. Oreste J. D'Aversa, "Reverend Rusty" as he is known informally, is an Inter-Faith (All-Faiths) Minister ordained by The New Seminary in New York City, New York.

He believes in the teachings of God, Jesus Christ, the Prophets, and the Ascended Masters. He is here to serve God and humankind to help make the world a better place for all people.

Reverend D'Aversa is an Author, Public Speaker, Spiritual Coach/Advisor and helps people find their true life's purpose and spiritual path. He is also a Business Coach, Consultant, Trainer and University Lecturer. He has appeared on radio and television as well as having his work featured in various newspapers and journals.

He is author of the following books:

- **Life Beyond the Pandemic: A Practical New Journey Handbook**
- **SELLING for NON-SELLING Professionals**
- **Baby Boomer Entrepreneur**

    (all available on Amazon.com)

His websites:

> www.GodLovesYouAndMe.org
> www.LifeBeyondThePandemic.com
> www.MetroSmallBusinessCoaching.com

He can be reached at:

> Email: OresteDAversa@outlook.com

NOTES

2. Introduction

Whether it is called a **Funeral Service** or a **Celebration of Life** it is a recognition of a person life here on Planet Earth. With all the current life events – the worldwide Pandemic, natural and man-made disasters, many people were and are not able to receive a proper Funeral Service or a Celebration of Life Service. Also, with the aforementioned situations, there may be shortages of Clergy and Funeral Directors to perform a proper Funeral Service or Celebration of Life Service.

I have written this book so that anyone can prepare and deliver a religious and/or spiritual, respectful and professional Funeral Service/Celebration of Life for Family Members, Friends and Loved Ones that have passed away and were not able to receive a proper service.

The book is designed in a simple to read and understand format with **Worksheets** at the end of the book for you to write your own Funeral Service or Celebration of Life Service.

The "Memorial Services Suggested Format" used in this book is a template to perform a service but as mentioned it is only a "Suggested Format". You can use it as is or "keep what you like and leave the rest". Each section will be defined with an example which you can use "as is" or can be modified to fit your needs. Then there be an area where you can write out your specific requirement for that section and at the end of the book there will be blank worksheets where you can put all the sections together to deliver your Funeral Service or Celebration of Life Service. You can take the book with you to deliver the ceremony at a specific location and read your ceremony you have written right out of this book.

What are 7 Purposes of a Funeral Service?
1. **Reality** – to accept the death of a loved one
2. **Acceptance** – the person is longer coming back.
3. **Recall** – to remember the person that has died in a respectful, loving and dignified manner.
4. **Support** – to provide active support to those that have lost someone through the grieving process.
5. **Expression** – to actively express our emotions to help in the healing process.

6. **Meaning** – to find meaning in the person's life and allow ourselves to find peace.
7. **Transcendence** – to helps us find a new self-identity. Funerals help us publicly mark a change in status.

May this guide help you during your time of sorrow and be a healing tool on your spiritual journey through the death of a loved one.

NOTES

3. Memorial Service

Below, as previous mentioned is the **Memorial Service Suggested Format**. It can be used "as is" or as to your specific needs require. You can take out items you feel you do not need, add items that are important to you or rearrange some of the items. The Memorial Service Suggested Format is a starting point to help you write a Funeral Service/Celebration of Life that is appropriate for you, your family, religious/spiritual background and more important appropriate for the person that has died.

I suggest that you write the **Memorial Service** when you are in a calm, reflective and meditative state of mind to express all your thoughts, feelings, and sentiments about the person you are doing the ceremony for. Writing a Memorial Service for an individual is a **sacred duty** to be done for the person that died, the people that knew that person and for GOD as we are all of GOD's creations.

Take your time. Write it out to the best of your ability. Sleep on it and review your Memorial Service to see if you have missed anything or want to add something more to it.

If you can't think of anything to write, ask GOD for some suggestions through prayer and meditation and GOD will supply you with what you need to know. If you get really into a jam, you can always go to the internet and ask Mr. Google for some help! 😊

Below I will go through each item of the **Memorial Service Suggested Format** briefly discuss and/or define it, provide an example, and have a blank area for you to write your own. At the end of the book, you can transfer all of your writings to blank worksheets that you can use, if you wish, to deliver the actual service at any location you choose.

To relieve stress, anxiety, and nervousness about delivering the service, I suggest you practice the service several times out loud to yourself even if it is to an empty room.

Memorial Service Suggested Format [16]

1. Opening Remarks/Introduction/Words of Welcome

2. Prayer of Invocation (Prayer to GOD)

3. Sacred Readings (Scripture, Readings with Special Meaning, Etc.)

4. Prayers

5. Musical Selections/Hymns

6. Formal Reading of Obituary

7. Moments of Silence/Meditation

8. Eulogy/Life Tribute

9. Brief Informal Life Tributes

10. Prayer of Thanksgiving for the Deceased's Life

11. Benediction (short blessing with which public worship is concluded)

12. Thank you and Acknowledgements

13. Closing Remarks

NOTES

1. Opening Remarks/Introduction/Words of Welcome

Purpose: To begin the Funeral Service/Celebration of Life and welcome attendees.

Sample(s): *"Welcome and thank you all for coming today. We are here today to honor a special person – **NAME OF PERSON**. No matter how much time I/we had to prepare for this day, I/we still do not feel ready to say goodbye."*

*"I/We appreciate how many of you have come to support me/us during this difficult time. Today will not be a traditional funeral service. Instead, we will have a Celebration of Life in honor of the joy **NAME OF PERSON** brought to so many people."*

1. Opening Remarks/Introduction/Words of Welcome

2. Prayer of Invocation

Purpose: An invocation prayer is an opening prayer for a service or meeting. Invocation prayers focus on worshipping GOD and seeking His presence in the gathering.

Sample(s): Beloved GOD, I pray that You bless us in the delivery of this Funeral Service/Celebration of Life for **NAME OF PERSON** and keep and protect us. GOD, let Your face shine on us and be gracious to us. We pray that we feel Your presence during this Funeral Service/Celebration of Life because You are with us wherever we go. We pray that this service focuses upon **NAME OF PERSON** well lived life. Amen.

2. Prayer of Invocation (Prayer to GOD)

3. Sacred Readings (Scripture, Readings with Special Meaning, Etc.)

Purpose: Reading from Sacred Texts (The Holy Bible, The Quran, etc.) that have meaning to this Funeral Service/Celebration of Life.

Sample(s): Psalm 23 (The Holy Bible)

The Lord is my shepherd; I shall not want.
2   He makes me lie down in green pastures.
He leads me beside still waters.
3   He restores my soul.
He leads me in paths of righteousness
    for his name's sake.
⁴ Even though I walk through the valley of the shadow of death,
    I will fear no evil,
for you are with me;
    your rod and your staff,
    they comfort me.
⁵ You prepare a table before me
    in the presence of my enemies;
you anoint my head with oil;
    my cup overflows.
⁶ Surely goodness and mercy shall follow me
    all the days of my life,
and I shall dwell in the house of the Lord
    forever.

Oh Soul At Rest, Return To Your Lord (The Quran)

"O soul that are at rest! Return to your Lord, well-pleased (with him), well-pleasing (Him), So enter among My servants, and enter into My garden." (Quran, 89:27-30)

3. Sacred Readings (Scripture, Readings with Special Meaning, Etc.)

_____

_____

_____

_____

_____

_____

_____

_____

_____

_____

_____

_____

_____

4. Prayers (See Chapter 4 for other Prayers)

Purpose: To offer prayers to God on behalf of the person being honored in the Funeral Service/Celebration of Life.

Sample(s): Funeral Blessing for a Loved One

May you always walk in sunshine,

and God's around you flow.

For the happiness you gave us,

No one will ever know.

It broke our hearts to lose you,

But you did not go alone.

A part of us went with you

The day God called you home.

A million times we needed you

A million times we cried.

If love could only have saved you

You would've never died.

The Lord be with you and may you rest in peace.

A Celtic Death Blessing by John O'Donohue

I pray that you will have the blessing of being consoled.

May you know in your soul that there is no need to be afraid.

When your time comes, may you be given every blessing and shelter that you need.

May there be a beautiful welcome for you in the home that you are going to.

You are not going somewhere strange.

You are going back to the home that you never left.

May you have a wonderful urgency to live your life to the full.

May you live compassionately and creatively and transfigure everything that is negative within you and about you.

When you come to die may it be after a long life.

May you be peaceful and happy and in the presence of those who really care for you.

May your going be sheltered and your welcome assured.

May your soul smile in the embrace of your anam cara (soul friend).

4. Prayers

4. Prayers

5. Musical Selections/Hymns

Purpose: **Hymns** are a meaningful choice of religious **music** that can be played at **funerals**. In addition to bringing peace and comfort for the grieving, **funeral hymns** stir memories strong memories of faith and tradition.

Sample(s): Amazing Grace

Amazing grace
How sweet the sound
That saved a wretch like me
I once was lost, but now I'm found
Was blind, but now I see
'Twas grace that taught my heart to fear
And grace my fears relieved
How precious did that grace appear
The hour I first believed
My chains are gone
I've been set free
My God, my Savior has ransomed me
And like a flood, His mercy rains
Unending love, Amazing grace
The Lord has promised good to me
His word my hope secures
He will my shield and portion be
As long as life endures
My chains are gone
I've been set free (been set free)
My God, my Savior has ransomed me (ransomed me)

And like a flood (like a flood) His mercy rains (mercy rains)
Unending love, oh, Amazing grace
The Earth shall soon dissolve like snow
The sun forbear to shine
But God, Who called me here below
Will be forever mine
My chains are gone
I've been set free
My God, my Savior has ransomed me
And like a flood, His mercy rains
Unending love, Amazing grace (grace)
I once was lost, but now I'm found
Was blind (was blind), but now (but now) I see

Ave Maria

Ave Maria
Gratia plena
Maria, gratia plena
Maria, gratia plena
Ave, ave dominus
Dominus tecum
Benedicta tu in mulieribus
Et benedictus
Et benedictus fructus ventris
Ventris tuae, Jesus.
Ave Maria
Ave Maria
Mater Dei
Ora pro nobis peccatoribus
Ora pro nobis
Ora, ora pro nobis peccatoribus
Nunc et in hora mortis

Et in hora mortis nostrae
Et in hora mortis nostrae
Et in hora mortis nostrae
Ave Maria

English translation:

Hail Mary, full of grace,
Mary, full of grace,
Mary, full of grace,
Hail, Hail, the Lord.
The Lord is with thee.
Blessed art thou among women, and blessed,
Blessed is the fruit of thy womb,
Thy womb, Jesus.
Hail Mary!
Hail Mary, Mother of God,
Pray for us sinners,
Pray, pray for us;
Pray, pray for us sinners,
Now and at the hour of our death,
The hour of our death
The hour of our death,
The hour of our death
Hail Mary.

5. Musical Selections/Hymns

6. Formal Reading of Obituary

Purpose: The obituary, like the funeral service, notifies the public of your loved one's passing. The purpose of an obituary is to notify the public of an individual's passing and relay the details of the services. It can also detail the life of the deceased.

Sample(s):
What Should Be Included?

- Announcement
- Biographical Information
- Survivors and Predeceased Information
- Scheduled Services
- Memorials
- Final Considerations

Obituary Samples

The following are fictitious examples of obituaries:

FORBES, Alex Downton

It is with great sadness that the family of Alex Downton Forbes announces his passing after a brief illness, on Saturday, April 3, 2014, at the age of 70 years. Alex will be lovingly remembered by his wife of 45 years, Joan and his children, Mike (Judy), Brad (Jill), Sue (Dan) Armandeau, and Ryan (Heidi). Bill will also be fondly remembered by his eight grandchildren, Brandy, Kala, Jack, Phillip, Jonah, Mackenzie, Paul and Austin, by his sisters, Ann (Joe) Kispinski, Eileen Rudolph and by sister-in-law Anne Forbes. Alex was predeceased by his brother Anton Forbes.

A Funeral Service in memory of Alex will be held on Thursday, April 7, 2014 at 1:00 p.m., at the Oliver's Funeral Home, 10005 - 107 Ave, Grande Prairie, with Rev. George Malcolm officiating. Interment will follow in the family plot at Emerson Trail Cemetery. Those who so desire may make memorial donations in memory of Alex to the (name and mailing address of foundation/society).

Riley, Laura (nee Gorman)

On Monday, February 3, 2014, Laura Riley, wife, mother, daughter and sister, passed away suddenly at the age of 36 years. Laura will be forever remembered by her husband and best friend Greg, and their precious children, Cody and Pamela, by her parents Jack and Ann Gorman, and by her brothers and sisters Andrew (Jill), Ken (Hope), Kim (Justin) Halow and Tianna (Wade) O'Halen. Andrea will also be forever remembered by her numerous nieces, nephews and extended family and dear friends.

A Prayer Service will be held on Thursday, February 6, at 7:00 p.m., at Oliver's Funeral Home, 10005 – 107 Ave, Grande Prairie.

A Mass of Christian Burial will be celebrated in memory of Laura on Friday, February 7, at 10:00 a.m., at St. Joseph's Catholic Church, 10404 - 102 Street, Grande Prairie, with Reverend Remi Hebert C.Ss.R. presiding.

Memorial donations in memory of Laura may be made to (name and mailing address of foundation/society).

6. Formal Reading of Obituary

7. Moments of Silence/Meditation

Purpose: To reflect in silence the life of the person that has died and to ponder our own lives on Earth.

Sample(s):

The meditation can be quiet time or the pondering of sacred scripture, hymn or anything that will help all attending reflect on the fragility of life and that we occupy this Earth for a short time.

7. Moments of Silence/Meditation

8. Eulogy/Life Tribute

Purpose: A eulogy is a speech given at a memorial service in memory of a person who has died. The purpose is to recall the defining qualities and highlights of a life lived in a way that benefits the audience, particularly the family.

Sample(s): Below is a Eulogy Template

Eulogy Template

Introduction

Childhood

Education & Career

Family

Hobbies

Commemorations

Conclusion

EULOGY EXAMPLE

Below is an example of the structure of a Eulogy.

In providing this, we aim to spark your creativity in writing part of the life story of your loved one.

Start off with what is provided below. On the following page you will find a blank template for you to fill in the blanks. Insert the details in brackets of your loved one and add as much extra detail as you like. The short sections provided are launching points to get you going in the right direction.

You may also like to begin or end with one of the scriptures, poems or readings from above.

INTRODUCTION

Today we gather to honor, remember, and say goodbye to **(NAME OF DECEASED PERSON)**.

Taking the words of a famous writer: "We make a living by what we get, we make a life by what we give". If that is true, then (name of deceased) made a great life. They were the most generous person I've ever known. I know many of you would agree judging from the nodding heads around the room.

CHILDHOOD

Our lives have all been touched by (**NAME OF DECEASED PERSON**) in some way, but you may not have known some details of their earlier life. (**NAME OF DECEASED PERSON**) was born (**FULL BIRTH NAME**) on (**THEIR BIRTH DATE**) in (**City**). He/She was the (**First, Second, only**) child of (**Name of loved one's Father**) and (**Name of loved one's Mother**). They lived in (**City**) from (**Year**) to (**Year**), and later moved to and (**Town**).

EDUCATION & CAREER

(**NAME OF DECEASED PERSON**) went to (**School**) and (Name of Schools) and graduated with (Name of Degree or Training). While studying at (School) (**NAME OF DECEASED PERSON**) was able to achieve (**List Achievements or Awards**). During this time (**NAME OF DECEASED PERSON**) became good friends with (**List of Friends Names**) and they remained good friends to this day.

He/She then went to work for (**Name of Company**) as a (**Name of Position**). Over the years, (**NAME OF DECEASED PERSON**) also worked for (**Company**), (**Company**) and (**Company**) OR also worked in (**Type of Job**). While working for (**Company**) (**NAME OF DECEASED PERSON**) was able to achieve (**List Achievements or Awards**).

FAMILY

In **(Year)** **(NAME OF DECEASED PERSON)** met **(Name of Spouse)** and they were married **(Number)** years later. Eventually they had **(Number)** children **(Names of their Children)**. Last year, **(NAME OF DECEASED PERSON)** and **(Spouse's Name)** celebrated their **(Number, e.g. 50th)** wedding anniversary.

HOBBIES

(NAME OF DECEASED PERSON) was very active in the **(Church, Community, Local Theatre, Quilting, Volunteer Firefighting)**. He/She devoted many hours to (hobby or service) and was known for **(what person was known for in the hobby or service, e.g. her exquisite quilt designs; always being ready with a helping hand; always having a positive attitude)**.

COMMEMORATIONS

I asked family and friends to tell me what they remember most about **(NAME OF DECEASED PERSON)**. There are so many good memories. **(List 5 or 6 memories in short sentence form, e.g. Playing music together. Fishing. His big hearty laugh. The time we went to Italy)**. One that I remember in particular is the time when **(tell a longer story that illustrates your loved one's personality – this can be a heart-warming story or a humorous story)**.

CONCLUSION

(NAME OF DECEASED PERSON) was a remarkably **(an adjective, e.g. good; thoughtful; hardworking; fun-loving) person.** He/She was a person of great **(two words that describe the person's character, e.g. devotion, integrity, love, compassion, service, humor).**

Above all, **(NAME OF DECEASED PERSON)** believed in **(The person's highest value, e.g. family, faith, hard work, independence, community, compassion).** He/She always said **(A common saying that illustrates the person's highest value, e.g. "family is the most important thing in life"; "you get out of life what you put into it"; "life is short, so enjoy it while you can!").**

Those are words of wisdom that I will always cherish.

In closing, I would like to share this poem with you:

<Use a poem, reading or scripture from above>

(NAME OF DECEASED PERSON), thank you for being part of our lives. We are all going to miss you deeply.

8. Eulogy/Life Tribute

_____
_____
_____
_____
_____
_____
_____
_____
_____
_____
_____
_____
_____
_____

9. Brief Informal Life Tributes

Purpose: Funerals are more about remembering the happy memories with a person who died than about being sad and saying goodbye. A Memorial Tribute helps comfort and may be delivered by friends and family members and support them during their grieving process.

Sample(s):

"The first thing I noticed about Sally was her big blonde, curly hair. It didn't take long to discover that her hair matched her personality. And it's that personality that I would like to celebrate with you today.

Let's start by remembering her laugh. I always knew where Sally was when I entered a restaurant for a lunch date with her and our high school friends. I only had to pause at the entrance of the dining room and listen for her loud, contagious laugh. I never had to wait long to hear it because Sally was always the life of the party."

9. Brief Informal Tributes

10. Prayer of Thanksgiving for the Deceased's Life

Purpose: To give thanks to GOD for the deceased's life.

Sample(s):

Eternal rest grant unto them, O Lord, and let perpetual light shine upon them. May the souls of the faithful departed through the mercy of God rest in peace. Amen.

Dear Heavenly Father, it is always hard to say goodbye to those that have died, for we know that they will be missed by so many who are left behind. But Lord, You also remind us that the death of Your saints is very special to You and we want to join together to thank You for life of this Your child, who was such an encouragement and wonderful witness of Your love and grace.

Thank You, Lord, for the blessings of this special person, whom we all remember so fondly, but who is now at rest in Your loving embrace. Thank You for their life and the many happy memories that we all share.

We pray that You will be a special comfort, to uplift and care for those that will feel the greatest loss. Help us to remember that although we are separated for a time, we will all rejoice one day when we stand together in Your presence. Thank You that the brief night of weeping will pass very quickly, and we will all be rejoicing in Your presence on that glorious morning when we will all be reunited in the hope that is set before us. In Jesus' name we pray,

Amen.

----

10. Prayer of Thanksgiving for the Deceased's Life

NOTES

11. Benediction (short blessing with which public worship is concluded)

Purpose: The short prayer at the end of a funeral service is actually for the funeral leader to pronounce a blessing of God on those attending and to ask for guidance in the days to come. A benediction is an official dismissal.

Sample(s):

"May the Lord bless you and keep you; the Lord make his face shine upon you and be gracious unto you; the Lord turn his face toward you and give you peace."

11. Benediction (short blessing with which public worship is concluded)

12. Thank you and Acknowledgements

Purpose: To show appreciation to all those that help you and your family dur the funeral process.

Sample(s):

"Our whole family thanks you all for all of your assistance during this very difficult time. Thank you for your love and very support through everything."

"Thank you, **NAME**, **NAME**, and **NAME**, for the **SPECIFIC THINGS THEY DID** to help our family. It meant a lot to us all and was a very big help."

"**NAME OF DECEASED**" would have loved your flowers, they were perfect. Thank you so much for such a beautiful contribution."

12. Thank you and Acknowledgements

13. Closing Remarks

Purpose: Closing statements in the Funeral Service/Celebration of Life Service

Sample(s):

The **NAME OF DECEASED** family and friends, thank you for joining us as the Saint Michael's community mourns the loss of Robert. Robert was one of the greatest storytellers we will ever know - a Utah voice whose plots and people, while they came to us from small and out-of-the-way places, spoke to all of us, whatever our life experiences. His themes were not limited by time and place - they were about our struggles with choices between good and evil in their everyday manifestations. Robert showed us that we do have choices, and that they are important, no matter how restricted our realm. And with his loving heart, discerning eye and keen sense of humor, Robert made us laugh while we absorbed these serious lessons.

Please join us at the Moonlight Diner for some food and storytelling - something that our beloved friend was a master at.

13. Closing Remarks

4. Funeral Prayers/Quotes

In this section there will be prayers by religion and spiritual traditions that can be used in your **Memorial Service,** or you can use your own. Some traditions are more a way of life rather than an organized religion, Confucianism, for example. For these types of situations meaningful Quotes will be used from their traditions.

a. African Religions [1]

**Praise Ye Lord,
Peace be with us.**

Say that the elders may have wisdom and speak with one voice.
Peace be with us.

Say that the country may have tranquility.
Peace be with us.

And the people may continue to increase.
Peace be with us.

Say that the people and the flock and the herds
May prosper and be free from illness.
Peace be with us.

Say that the fields may bear much fruit
And the land may continue to be fertile.
Peace be with us.

May peace reign over earth,
May the gourd cup agree with vessel.
Peace be with us.

May their heads agree and every ill word be driven out
Into the wilderness, into the virgin forest.

– Kikuyu Peace Prayer –

http://www.godprayers.org/Kikuyu-Peace-Prayer.html

Great is O King,
our happiness
in thy kingdom,
thou, our king.

We dance before thee,
our king,
by the strength
of thy kingdom.

May our feet
be made strong.
let us dance before thee,
eternal.

Give ye praise,
all angels,
to him above
who is worthy of praise.

– Zulu, South Africa –

http://www.dailyom.com/library/000/000/000000461.html

Agbegi lere, la'fin ewu l'ado,
He who carves the cloth at Ado in the form of a sculpture,

Eiti Olodumare ko pa'jo iku e da,
The one whose date of death
has not been changed by the wind,

Omo Oluworiogbo,
Child of the Chief Priest who made
all the Heads that exist in Creation.

Iba'se ila Oorun,
Homage to the power of East,

Iba'se iwo Oorun,
Homage to the power of the West,

Iba'se Ariwa,
Homage to the power of the North,

Iba'se Guusu,
Homage to the power of the South,

Iba Oba Igbalaye,
Homage to the King of the Seasons of the Earth,

Iba Orun Oke,
Homage to the Invisible Realm of the Mountains,

Iba Atiwo Orun,
Homage to all things that live in the Invisible Realm,

Iba Okiti biri, Oba ti np'ojo iku da,

Homage to the Averter of the final days,
The King who could change the time of Death,

Iba ate-ika eni Olodumare,
Homage to the mat that cannot be rolled up once laid out,

Iba Odemu demu kete a lenu ma fohun,
Homage to the power that extracts Goodness
from the Realm of the Invisible,

Iba'se awon Iku emese Orun,
Homage to the dead, the messengers of the Invisible Realm.

– Iba'se, Parts of the Ifa Prayer of Praise, West Africa –

NOTES

b. Bahá'í Faith [2]

Prayer for the Dead

(The Prayer for the Dead is the only Bahá'í obligatory prayer that is to be recited in congregation; it is to be recited by one believer while all present stand in silence. Bahá'u'lláh has clarified that this prayer is required only when the deceased is over the age of fifteen, that its recital must precede interment, and that there is no requirement to face the Qiblih during its recitation. "Alláh-u-Abhá" is said once; then the first of the six verses is recited nineteen times. Then "Alláh-u-Abhá" is said again, followed by the second verse, which is recited nineteen times, and so on.)

O my God! This is Thy servant and the son of Thy servant who hath believed in Thee and in Thy signs, and set his face towards Thee, wholly detached from all except Thee. Thou art, verily, of those who show mercy the most merciful.

Deal with him, O Thou Who forgivest the sins of men and concealest their faults, as beseemeth the heaven of Thy bounty and the ocean of Thy grace. Grant him admission within the precincts of Thy transcendent mercy that was before the foundation of earth and heaven. There is no God but Thee, the Ever-Forgiving, the Most Generous.

Let him, then, repeat six times the greeting "Alláh-u-Abhá," and then repeat nineteen times each of the following verses:

We all, verily, worship God.

We all, verily, bow down before God.

We all, verily, are devoted unto God.

We all, verily, give praise unto God.

We all, verily, yield thanks unto God.

We all, verily, are patient in God.

(If the dead be a woman, let him say: This is Thy handmaiden and the daughter of Thy handmaiden, etc...)

---

c. Buddhism [3]

1. "Tibetan Dying Prayer"

Through your blessing, grace, and guidance, through the power of the light that streams from you:
May all my negative karma, destructive emotions, obscurations, and blockages be purified and removed,
May I know myself forgiven for all the harm I may have thought and done,
May I accomplish this profound practice of phowa, and die a good and peaceful death,
And through the triumph of my death, may I be able to benefit all other beings, living or dead.

----

2. "A Buddhist Prayer for Peace"

May all beings everywhere plagued with sufferings of body and mind quickly be freed from their illnesses.
May those frightened cease to be afraid, and may those bound be free.

May the powerless find power and may people think of befriending one another.

May those who find themselves in trackless, fearful wildernesses—the children, the aged, the unprotected—be guarded by beneficent celestials, and may they swiftly attain Buddhahood.

----

3. "Traditional Buddhist Blessing and Healing Chant"

Just as the soft rains fill the streams,
Pour into the rivers and join together in the oceans,
So may the power of every moment of your goodness
Flow forth to awaken and heal all beings,
Those here now, those gone before, those yet to come.

By the power of every moment of your goodness
May your heart's wishes be soon fulfilled
As completely shining as the bright full moon,
As magically as by a wish-fulfilling gem.

By the power of every moment of your goodness
May all dangers be averted and all disease be gone.
May no obstacle come across your way.
May you enjoy fulfillment and long life.

For all in whose heart dwells respect,
Who follow the wisdom and compassion, of the Way,
May your life prosper in the four blessings
Of old age, beauty, happiness, and strength.

----

d. Christianity [4]

Prayer for the Dead

God our Father,
Your power brings us to birth,
Your providence guides our lives,
and by Your command we return to dust.

Lord, those who die still live in Your presence,
their lives change but do not end.
I pray in hope for my family,
relatives and friends,
and for all the dead known to You alone.

In company with Christ,
Who died and now lives,
may they rejoice in Your kingdom,
where all our tears are wiped away.
Unite us together again in one family,
to sing Your praise forever and ever.

Amen.

Cemetery Prayer # 2

In sure and certain hope of the resurrection to eternal life
through Our Lord Jesus Christ,
we commend to Almighty God **(Name),**
and we commit his/her body to the ground:
earth to earth,
ashes to ashes,
dust to dust.

The Lord bless him/her and keep him/her,
the Lord make His Face to shine upon him/her
and be gracious to him/her,
the Lord lift up His countenance upon him/her
and give him/her peace.

Amen.

Cemetery Prayer # 3

O God, this hour revives in us memories of loved ones
who are here no more.
What happiness we shared when they walked among us!
What joy, when, loving and loved,
we lived our lives together!
Their memory is a blessing forever.

Months or years may have passed,
yet we feel near to them.
Our hearts yearn for them.
Though the bitter grief has softened,
a duller pain abides,
for the place where once they stood is empty now.
The links of life are broken,
but the links of love and longing cannot break.
Their souls are bound up with ours forever.

O Lord, I thank You
for allowing me to have these very special people in my life.

I have been truly blessed by their presence,
their words and actions, and their love.
I grieve not for them, but for myself, as I truly miss them.
We shared so much,
and yet I feel our times together were fleeting.
Help me, O God,
to realize that the distance between us now
is not so great and that one day,
I will be reunited with them in paradise.
Together, we will glorify You,
Almighty Father, Your only Son, Jesus Christ,
and Your Holy Spirit for all eternity.

Amen.

NOTES

e. Confucianism [5]

Death and life have their determined appointments riches and honors depend upon heaven.

-Confucius

If we don't know life, how can we know death?

-Confucius

Heaven means to be one with God.

-Confucius

NOTES

f. Hinduism [6]

At Hindu funerals, prayers are meant to celebrate the deceased and give comfort to the living. Traditional funeral prayers blend both aspects of life and often combine the recite of Hindu mantras to help those living stay conscious.

ANTYESTI

This traditional rite of passage, literally means "last sacrifice" and is often recited at Hindu funerals.

Burn him not up, nor quite consume him, Agni: let not his body or his skin be scattered,

O all possessing Fire, when thou hast matured him, then send him on his way unto the Fathers.

When thou hast made him ready, all possessing Fire, then do thou give him over to the Fathers,

When he attains unto the life that waits him, he shall become subject to the will of gods.

The Sun receive thine eye, the Wind thy Prana (life-principle, breathe); go, as thy merit is, to earth or heaven.

Go, if it be thy lot, unto the waters; go, make thine home in plants with all thy members.

— Rigveda 10.16

NOTES

g. Islam [7]

ISLAMIC FUNERAL PRAYERS

When someone of Islamic faith passes away, Muslims within the community often gather to offer prayers for the deceased's forgiveness.

SALAT-E-JENAZA OR NAMAZE JENAZA

This prayer is offered in a specific way with a few Takbirs, which literally means "God is greater," every Muslim adult male must perform the funeral prayer upon the death of any Muslim.

The prayer begins with the first takbir of Allaho Akbarby Iman.

Glory be to you Oh Allah, and praise be to You, and blessed is Your name, and exalted is Your Majesty, and there is none to be served besides You.

Then, the Iman says the second takbir of Allaho Akbar.

Oh Allah! Send grace and honor on Mohammad and on the family and true followers of Mohammad just as you sent Grace and Honor on Ibrahim and on the family and his true followers. Surely, you are praiseworthy, the Great."

The Iman Say Allaho Akbar, is the third takbir.

Oh Allah! Forgive of us who are alive and those of who are dead; those of us who are present and those of us who are absent' those of us who are young and those of us who are adults; our males and our females. O 'Allah! Whomsoever You keep alive, let him live as a follower of Islam and whomsoever You cause to die, let him die as a believer.

This ends the Salat-e-Jenaza or namaze Jenaza for adults.

THE FUNERAL PRAYER

If the deceased is an adult, male or female, the following Prayer is recited:

O. Allah, forgive our living ones and our deceased ones and those of us who are present and those who are absent, and our young ones and our old ones and our males and our females.

O Allah those of us whom Thou grantest life, keep them firm on Islam, and those of us whom Thou causest to die, cause them to die in the faith. Deprive us not, O Allah, of the benefits relating to the deceased and subject us not to trial after him.

The particular prayer for a deceased male child:

O Allah make him our forerunner, and make him, for us, a reward and a treasure, and make him for us a pleader and accept his pleading.

Particular prayer for a deceased female child:

O Allah makes her our forerunner, and makes her, for us, a reward and a treasure, and make her for us a pleader and accept her pleading.

NOTES

h. Jainism [8]

Namokar Mantra

(These five salutations evaporate and eradicate negative influences. This is the most sacred and auspicious prayer of all Jaina prayers.

With some versions 'Om' is recited at the beginning of the first four lines.

Notes on pronunciations:
- 'A' is pronounced as 'u' as in 'but'
- 'AA' is a long 'aw' sound as in 'saw')

(OM) NAMO ARIHANTAANAM
I bow to the Jinas (Arhants) the Perfected, yet Embodied Souls, possessed of Infinite Consciousness, Energy and Happiness;

(OM) NAMO SIDDHAANAM
I bow to the Perfect, Pure (Free of Karmic Attachments), Liberated Souls (Siddhas), those who have attained Moksha,;

(OM) NAMO AAYARIYAANAM
I bow to the Ascetic Leaders (Aacharyas) of the Jaina Order;

(OM) NAMO UVAJJHAAYAANAM
I bow to the Ascetic Preceptors/Teachers (Upadhyayas);

NAMO LOAE SAVVA SAAHUUNAM

I bow to all the Jaina Ascetics (Monks/Nuns) in the world devoted to Purification of Soul/Self.

ESO PANCHA NAMOKAARO
SAVVA PAAVA PANAASANO
MANGALAANAM CHA SAVVESIM
PADHAMAM HAVAI MANGALAM

Kshamaapanaa Sutra

KHAAMEMII SAVVE JIVAA
SAVVE JIVAA KHAMANTU ME
METTI ME SAVVE BHUESUU
VERAM MAJJHAM
NA KENAI.

I grant forgiveness to all living beings;
and may all of them forgive me.
I have friendship with all living beings;
and hostility toward none.

Words of Assurance

Anyone who recognizes their divine self is a new creation.
The old life has gone; a new life has begun.
Friends, believe in the truth and nature of the indestructible, pure Soul; and be at peace.

Prayer for Sending Forth

Living beings are comprised of two substances: material particles and Soul.
The bodies of living beings are mortal, formed from particles of matter.

And to particles of matter these bodies must return.
This is an inescapable law of nature (or 'of the universe').
The Soul is immortal.
Thus even in death we recognize that life continues, with opportunity for continued and
increased happiness.
May the Soul of _____ be now in a place where there is neither pain nor
sorrow nor dying. Where it can continue to make progress toward Moksha/Liberation; when
there is eternal bliss and forevermore freedom from the suffering of the cycle of birth, death
and rebirth.
Shuddha A–tm–a, Shuddha A–tm–a, Shuddha A–tm–.
Pure Soul, Pure Soul, Pure Soul

NOTES

i. Judaism [9]

Mourner's Kaddish

Kaddish prayers are a cornerstone of Judaism. They provide an opportunity for mourners to praise God's name and acknowledge their pain. The term comes from an Aramaic word which means 'holy.' This praise is obvious in an excerpt of the prayer:

"May His great name be kept magnified and sanctified in the world that is to be created anew, where He will revive the dead, and raise them up to eternal life; and rebuild the city of Jerusalem; and establish His Temple in its midst; and uproot alien worship from the earth and restore the worship of Heaven to its place. May the Holy One, blessed be He, reign in His sovereignty and glory, during your life ring your days."

The Kaddish provides hope. In the Jewish faith, God will resurrect the righteous to experience eternal life. This allows mourners to believe that they will see their loved ones again. The Kaddish also serves as a guide through many complex stages of grief. One of the issues with a Western approach to grief is speed.

Grief makes people uncomfortable. It's hard to cope with. The bereaved 'should' sweep all their emotions under the rug as soon as possible. It's even a subject of praise. Mentioning how 'strong' someone is, or how 'well they're holding up' is common in Western culture.

This can make someone feel like everyone has forgotten the deceased. They may feel that they're expected to move on as if nothing happened. In Judaism, this isn't the case. When a close relative passes away, a Kaddish is recited by mourners for eleven months. This allows a slow transition back into the ordinary world.

El Maleh Rachamim (Jewish Prayer of the Dead)

The phrase 'el maleh rachamim' translates to 'God full of compassion'. Indeed, this prayer is a call to God's compassionate nature. In Jewish thought, souls go to paradise after death.

This prayer pleads with God to give them rest and contentment in the next world. Asking God to have mercy is a tradition in the Jewish faith. An excerpt from the prayer demonstrates this:

"Oh God, full of compassion, who dwells on high, grant true rest upon the wings of the Divine Presence, in the exalted spheres of the holy and pure ... Therefore, may the All-Merciful One shelter him with the cover of His wings forever, and bind his soul in the bond of life. The Lord is his heritage, may he rest in his resting-place in peace; and let us say: Amen."

Psalm 90

The Psalms are a cornerstone of the Jewish liturgy and faith. They express a broad range of emotions. From anger with God to heart-stopping sorrow, to endless joy, the Psalms are a form of human expression. The extent of emotions they discuss is why they are commonly used in funerals.

"My protector, You are our abode, one generation to the next, Since before the mountains came to birth, before the birth pangs of the land and world. From eternity to eternity, You are divine. Truly, a thousand years are in your eyes like yesterday--so quickly does it pass--or like the watchman's nighttime post. You pour upon them sleep, they sleep … At dawn, life blossoms and renews itself; at dusk, it withers and dries up."

King David, a figure who experienced much personal loss, is said to have written many of these Psalms.

NOTES

j. Native American [10]

Great Spirit Prayer

Oh, Great Spirit,
Whose voice I hear in the winds
and whose breath gives life to all the world.
Hear me! I need your strength and wisdom.
Let me walk in beauty, and make my eyes
ever hold the red and purple sunset.
Make my hands respect the things you have made
and my ears sharp to hear your voice.
Make me wise so that I may understand
the things you have taught my people.
Let me learn the lessons you have hidden
in every leaf and rock.

Help me remain calm and strong in the
face of all that comes towards me.
Help me find compassion without
empathy overwhelming me.
I seek strength, not to be greater than my brother,
but to fight my greatest enemy: myself.
Make me always ready to come to you
with clean hands and straight eyes.
So when life fades, as the fading sunset,
my spirit may come to you without shame.

- Translated by Lakota Sioux Chief Yellow Lark in 1887

Prayer for Life

Our old women gods, we ask you!
Our old women gods, we ask you!
Then give us long life together,
May we live until our frosted hair is white;
May we live till then.
This life that now we know!

- Tewa (North American Indian) Traditional Prayer

A Chinook Prayer

May all I say and all I think
be in harmony with thee,
God within me,
God beyond me,
maker of the trees.

- Chinook prayer, Pacific Northwest Coast

---

k. Pagan [11]

Funeral Prayers

May your soul take a soft-footed journey,
on a soft-floored path through the old forest
to the Land of Comfort,
where the only tears are the drops of rain falling from leaves,
the only moaning deep ocean swells,
the only sighing light evening breezes.
Rest in that land, with the peace you have earned.

To the person who has died, we say:
"Peace between us; go on your way with our blessing."
To those who have come here for farewells, we say:
"Peace among us; may we live blessed together."

The Goddess

His/her whole life has been like waiting and growing in the womb.
The time has come for his/her birth, from this world into another.
Bring him/her, Goddess, through the pangs of this new birth,
thereinto that other world.
Hold your baby there, draw him/her close to you, feeding him/her with inexhaustible milk from your ever giving breasts.

Rock him/her in your soothing arms, until he/she knows the peace of a baby resting in his complete faith in his/her mother.

----

l. Shinto [12]

THE PRAYER

A life has ended, with the passing of a friend,
the memories of times, have come to an end,
their threads wove the fabric of an earlier day.

A life has ended, with the passing of a friend,
sunrises and sunsets, bright days and dark nights
circled again and again, and gave context to this life,
moment after moment, their life was lived each day.

A life has ended, with the passing of a friend,
lives have been touched by the dear one's journey,
laughter, tears, hopes, fears, a life has come to an end
memories hold their spirit alive, in my own life.

A life has ended, with the passing of a friend,
the loss of future moments, that will not be,
grateful for moments shared, that nourished me,
moments lived, in casual belief, they would never end.

A part of me has ended, with the passing of a friend,
be they gone from the earthly plane, their spirit soars,
to renew again, in summerland, heaven or another life,
I know not where, but their love remains with me,
for in this life, we friends, did share.

I miss my friend, but they will always be near, inside
of me, inside you, and all who took time to hear,
the music of this life so dear, a life now silent,
living only in the memory, of those who survive.

NOTES

m. Sikhism [13]

Shabads

Shabads are hymns in the Sikh religion. This could refer to the hymns in the Holy Text, the main scripture for Sikhs. It can also be another term for God.

Shabads are commonly read or even sang at funerals. These focus on feelings of hope and healing, so they're powerful for family members. There are no funeral songs, only shabad hymns. While the family could choose their own favorites to read upon the death of a loved one, these are the most common:

- Jeevan Maran Sukh Ho-e
- Jot Milee Sang Jot
- Sooraj Kiran Milae
- Oudhak Samund Salal Kee

Death Prayers

There are many different death prayers recited at the time of death. Prayer plays a significant role in the Sikh tradition and brings families closer to God, from prayers at the dying's bedside to final funeral prayers.

The most common death prayer is the Kirtan Sohila. This is a nighttime prayer in Sikhism. The name itself translates to "Song of Praise." This is traditionally recited at the end of an evening ceremony, but it's also a standard part of the funeral procession.

Because this is a nighttime prayer, it symbolizes the end of the soul's cycle on Earth, no unlike the sun setting after a long day.

Kirtan Sohila

The bedtime prayer, Kirtan Sohila is usually recited just before sleeping at night. It's name means 'Song of Peace'. Kirtan Sohila is composed of five hymns, the first three by Guru Nanak Dev, the fourth by Guru Ram Das and the fifth by Guru Arjan Dev. This hymn is usually recited at the conclusion of evening ceremonies at the Gurdwara and also recited as part of Sikh funeral services.

Gauri Dipaki Measure, Guru Nanak

God is only One, He is obtained by the Grace of the True Guru.

In whatever house (state of mind) meditation on God is practiced and His praises are snug,

Sing His praises and meditate upon Him in that house.

You, please, sing the praises of my God, the Fearless.

I am a sacrifice to the Song which gives perpetual peace.

Every day, God looks after and beholds all the beings.

None can assess the price of Your Gifts, so how can the Giver be assessed?

The day and hour of the marriage (departure to the next world) is fixed, so the friends should pour the customary oil on the threshold.

Bless the bride, so that union with the Master, may be obtained.

Such calls and summons to reach the next world are sent to every house, every day.

Nanak reminds: meditate on the One, Who sends calls; that day will come soon.

Asa Measure, Guru Nanak

There are six shastras (books of Hindu thought), their six authors and six methods of teaching;

But One God alone is the Teacher of teachers, though He manifests Himself in many ways.

O God! by that religious books way by which your praises are sung is the best,

Follow that way, which glorifies God.

Just as seconds, minutes, hours, quarters of a day, lunar days, week days, months,

Are created by one sun and so are created many seasons by it,

Similarly God, Who is One has many manifestations, so says Nanak.

Dhanasri Measure, Guru Nanak

The sky is the salver; the sun and the moon the lamps; the stars, with their orbs, are the studed pearls.

The fragrance of sandalwood is the incense, the wind the fan and all vegetation are flowers.

Thus Your Wonderful Worship is performed my God! O, the Destroyer of Fears, this is Your true worship with true lamps.

The Unstruck Melody rings and the Divine Music of the Shabad (Word) is the tender flute.

Your eyes are thousands, yet You have no eye; Your forms are thousands, yet You have no form.

Your pure feet are thousands, yet You have no feet; You are without nose, yet You have a thousand noses; Your plays have, in this way, bewitched me.

The same Light pervades all.

This Light causes the light to shine within all.

Through the Gurus advice the divine Light becomes visible.

That, which pleases Him, constitutes His real worship.

My soul bewitched by the Lotus Feet (Divine Hymns) of God, as sweet as honey, for which I am thirsty day and night.

Nanak says: Give the water of Your Mercy to this pied cuckoo, so that I may merge in Your Name.

Gauri Purbi Measure, Guru Ram Das

Lust and anger completely fill this town body; but these have been smashed to pieces by meeting the Saint (Guru).

I have met the Guru, because of my predestined luck and I have intered the sphere of Gods Love.

Salute the True saint with folded hands, this is a great virtuous act.

Lie prostrate before Him, this is a great virtuous act.

Lovers of mammon do not enjoy the taste of Gods Elixir, as within them there is the thorn of ego.

When they walk forward, that thorn pricks them more and more severly; they suffer greater pain and finally receive on their heads, the blows from deaths staff.

True devotees are absorbed in Gods Name, and fear of the pain of birth and deaths leaves them.

They are united with the Everlasting God and gain great honour in the various regions and universes.

O God! the Greatest of the great, save us, we are poor and humble.

Nanak says: the Name is the Sustainer and support of the mortal, and gives Supreme Joy and peace.

Gauri Purbi Measure, Guru Arjan Dev

My friend, I request you that this is the opportune time to serve the saints.

Earn divine profits in this world and live in peace and comfort in the next one.

Life is shortening day and night.

O mind, meet the Guru and set right your affairs.

This world is engrossed in sins and evils; but Gods Divines will swim across it.

He, who is awakened by God, drinks the Nectar of Name and comes to realise the Ineffable God.

Purchase the commodity, for which you have come in this world, and then God will come to reside in your heart with the Gurus Grace.

You will easily obtain your Real Home and will not suffer transmigration.

O Searcher of hearts and Fulfiller of desires! kindly fulfil my hearts desires.

Nanak says: I, your servant, pray that I may become the dust of the Saints feet join the society of saints.

NOTES

n. Taoism [14]

Taoist Prayers

Prayers inspired by those who practice the religious or philosophical tradition of living with the Tao or "The Way."

Disciples of Life

We are born gentle and weak. At death we are hard and stiff. Green plants are tender and filled with sap. When they die they are withered and dry. Therefore the stiff and unbending are the disciples of death. The gentle and yielding are the disciples of life.

- Lao Tzu from the "Tao Te Ching"

Lao-tsu's Peace Prayer

If there is to be peace in the world,
There must be peace in the nations.

If there is to be peace in the nations,
There must be peace in the cities.

If there is to be peace in the cities,
There must be peace between neighbors.

If there is to be peace between neighbors,
There must be peace in the home.

If there is to be peace in the home,
There must be peace in the heart.

- Lao-tsu

Balance Prayer

Lord, let us empty of all doctrines,
The Tao is wisdom eternally inexhaustible.
Fathomless for the mere intellect,
The Tao is the law wherewith all things come into being.

It blunts the edges of the intellect,
Untangles the knots of the mind,
Softens the glare of thinking,
And settles the dust of thought.

Transparent yet invisible,
The Tao exists like deep pellucid water.
Its origin is unknown,
For it existed before Heaven and Earth.

- Lao-tsu

---

o. Zoroastrianism [15]

Funeral (Geh Saania) Ceremony:

At the service and while at the funeral home, a table holding a Iit deevo, the picture of Zarathustra, and flowers may be kept. On a separate table or area, photographs of the deceased during his/her UK time may be appropriate. Some may also prefer playing somber music during the wake or before the funeral service begins. The main part of the ritual of the funeral ceremony is known as Geh Saarna meaning chanting of the Gathas. The Gathas are a set of live divinely inspired hymns composed by prophet Zarathustra. They contain the simple and universal teachings of the Zarathushti religion. The main content of the Geh Saarna prayer is the chanting of the Ahunavaiti Gatha (first of the five Gathas in the ancient language of Avesta. The Ahunavaiti Gatha is recited to comfort and soothe the Soul in the initial stage of its journey to the spiritual world. A Iit deevo (oil lump) or candle is kept on a table near the head side of the casket. Two priests generally perform this ceremony: however, if priests are not available, the ceremony can be performed by any Zarathushti. The two people performing the ceremony cleanse their hands and face with water and complete the Kushti ritual. They then stand a few feet from the body holding two ends of a clean piece of white cloth to maintain paiwand. This implies a close spiritual connection between them and symbolizes a Joint effort with increased strength of the recitation of the prayers.

The translations of some selected verses from the Ahunavaiti Gatha are presented below:

(From the book titled The Teachings of Zarathushtra The Prophet of Iran on How to Think and Succeed in life by T.R. Sethna)

Ha (Chapter) 28 Verse 1:

With uplifted hands and deep humility. I beseech, O Mazda, first and foremost this, the abiding joy of Spenta Mainyu, your holy mind. Grant that I perform all actions in harmony with righteousness (Your Divine Law), and acquire the wisdom of the good mind so that I may bring happiness to the Soul of the Universe.

(The above verse is recited at the start of the first Ha and at the end of each of the seven Has of the Ahunavad Gatha).

Ha (Chapter) 28 Verse 2:

O Ahura Mazda, may I reach you in fullness of knowledge. Through good mind, to be graced with realization of both the selves, the physical (lower) self and the mental (higher) self which comes from following your divine law, through which you lead all devotees into the abode of light (Heaven).

Ha (Chapter) 28 Verse 3:

I shall weave songs of adoration, as was never done before for you O Righteousness, and for you O Good Mind, and for you O Mazda Ahura, for through you flourishes divine wisdom and the never waning moral courage. So descend. O Powers, in answer to these invocations and grant us Perfect Bliss.

Ha (Chapter) 28 Verse 4:<.H4>

In truth when singing your praise. I shall attune my Soul to good thoughts and become aware of the blessings which flow from holy deeds undertaken for Mazda Ahura's sake. As long as I have the will and strength, so long I will teach mankind to strive for righteousness.

Ha (Chapter) 29 Verse 11:

When would I attain righteousness, good thoughts and moral courage? O Mazda, on account of equity, ennoble this great brotherhood. O Ahura, we need your blessings for our protection.

Ha (Chapter) 30 Verse 1:

Now I shall proclaim to those who have assembled here, all that is to be learned from Mazda, viz., the hymns of the Lord, the praises of good mind and what noble principled righteousness is, which by its light points out the real bliss.

Ha (Chapter) 30 Verse 2:

Hear the best (Truth) with your ears and decide by your pure mind. Let everybody judge for his own self and find out what he ought to do. Before the great trial let all wake up to this my counsel.

Ha (Chapter) 30 Verse 9:

And may we be like those who have prospered the world, chosen righteousness and the brotherhood of Ahura Mazda. May mind and heart turn in unison to You whenever our reason is overwhelmed with doubt.

Ha (Chapter) 31 Verse 4:

Ahura Mazda, in order that righteousness may be ideal to live for. I desire the excellent divine wisdom, the best of good thoughts and the mighty moral courage with whose help I would overcome untruth.

Ha (Chapter) 33 Verse 12:

Reveal yourself within me. O Ahura, and through divine wisdom grant me desire for perfection through your devotion, O Mazda, grant me goodness as reward for prayers, through righteousness the full vigor of Soul and all embracing love through good thoughts.

Ha (Chapter) 34 Verse 15:

Therefore, O Mazda, you teach me the noblest words and deeds by which I may in truth fulfill my earnest desire of my prayers, achieving it through the good mind and righteousness, O Ahura, through your power (Moral Strength) regenerate my life as you wish it is true.

At the conclusion of the prayers, family members or friends may address the congregation if the family so desires. The congregation pays their last respects and the casket is removed to the disposal site. In North America, cremation is the preferred mode of disposal of the body. The mode of burial is considered to contaminate the earth, is therefore deemed undesirable. It is customary to consign the ashes from the cremation back to nature. In the US, after the funeral service the body in the casket is carried by Funeral Personnel or by family members and friends to the hearse and driven to the cremation site. A funeral procession with cars (head lights on) follows the hearse. At the crematorium the person is given his/her last respects and the priests pray final Kusti prayers and Sarosh Baj. The body is then handed over to the crematorium personnel who then process it for cremation. In the USA close relatives and friends return to the home of the deceased to comfort the family. Before entering the house, Parsis wash their hands and sprinkle water as a ceremonial bath and do their Kusti prayers.

Refreshments may be served for the guests attending the services. According to Parsi customs, relatives and friends avoid eating meal for three days. On the fourth day, the Uthamna ceremony is performed when the Soul is judged and passes over to the other world.

NOTES

5. Conclusion

I hope this guide was helpful in preparing your Funeral Service/Celebration of Life Ceremony for the special person/people in your life.

Hopefully you found the Memorial Service Suggested Template, Prayers/Quotes and Worksheets useful in putting together a meaningful, respectful, and professional Funeral Service/Celebration of Life Ceremony to fulfill your needs.

As previously mentioned, the book was designed in a simple to read and understand format with Worksheets at the end of the book for you to write your own Funeral Service or Celebration of Life Service.

As to not be overwhelmed when writing/preparing the Funeral Service/Celebration of Life Ceremony, if time permits, I suggest you write some of the service, take a break and/or sleep on it and look at it with a "fresh set of eyes" the next day. Should you get overwhelmed by any of this – take a break, get some fresh air, and never forget God is always there for help. Never forget, God will find a way where there appears to be no way…

I sincerely hope this guide helps you through your journey at a difficult time in your life.

May GOD bless you and send you, your family and friends' strength, comfort, and love!

NOTES

NOTES

NOTES

6. Worksheets

NOTES

Memorial Service Worksheets

1. Opening Remarks/Introduction/Words of Welcome

_____

_____

_____

_____

_____

_____

_____

_____

_____

_____

_____

_____

_____

_____

NOTES

2. Prayer of Invocation (Prayer to GOD)

NOTES

3. Sacred Readings (Scripture, Readings with Special Meaning, Etc.)

_____

_____

_____

_____

_____

_____

_____

_____

_____

_____

_____

_____

_____

_____

_____

_____

_____

NOTES

4. Prayers

NOTES

5. Musical Selections

NOTES

6. Formal Reading of Obituary

NOTES

7. Moments of Silence/Meditation

NOTES

8. Eulogy/Life Tribute

NOTES

9. Brief Informal Life Tributes

NOTES

10. Prayer of Thanksgiving for the Deceased's Life

NOTES

11. Benediction (short blessing with which public worship is concluded)

NOTES

12. Thank you and Acknowledgements

NOTES

13. Closing Remarks

NOTES

Memorial Service (Blank Worksheets)

1. _____

2.

3.

4.

5.

6.

7.

8. _____

9. _____

10.

11.

12.

13.

NOTES

7. Footnotes

4. Prayers

a. African Religions [1]

Africa Prayers for the Dead

https://tersiaburger.com/2013/10/19/africa-prayers-for-the-dead/

---

b. Bahá'í Faith [2]

Prayer for the Dead

https://www.bahaiprayers.org/depart1.htm

---

c. Buddhism [3]

3 Short Buddhist Prayers for the Dead, Dying or Sick

https://www.joincake.com/blog/buddhist-prayer-for-the-dead/

---

d. Christianity [4]

Prayers for the Dead

https://www.catholic.org/prayers/prayer.php?p=805

---

e. Confucianism [5]

MeaningIn.com

https://meaningin.com/confucius/death/quotes

---

f. Hinduism [6]

HINDU FUNERAL PRAYERS

https://www.thegardens.com/traditional-funeral-prayers/

---

g. Islam [7]

ISLAMIC FUNERAL PRAYERS

https://www.thegardens.com/traditional-funeral-prayers/

THE FUNERAL PRAYER

https://amjfuneralservices.ca/54/The-Funeral-Prayer.html

---

h. Jainism [8]

India (Jainism)

https://cog.org/wp-content/uploads/2015/10/India-Jainism.pdf

---

i. Judaism [9]

10 Popular Jewish Funeral Prayers and Poems

https://www.joincake.com/blog/jewish-funeral-prayers/

---

j. Native American [10]

JesuitResource.org

https://www.xavier.edu/jesuitresource/online-resources/prayer-index/native-american

---

k. Pagan [11]

A Book of Pagan Prayer

https://documents.pub/download/a-book-of-pagan-ritual-prayerpdf

---

l. Shinto [12]

Prayers.co.uk

https://www.prayers.co.uk/shinto/death-prayer2.html

---

m. Sikhism [13]

Sikh Funerals (Antam Sanskar): Customs, Attire & What to Expect

https://www.joincake.com/blog/sikh-funeral/

Sikhs.org

https://www.sikhs.org/transl6.htm

---

n. Taoism [14]

JusuitResource.org

https://www.xavier.edu/jesuitresource/online-resources/prayer-index/taoist-prayers

---

o. Zoroastrianism [15]

Zoroastrian Rituals and Geh Saarnaa Prayer

http://www.avesta.org/ritual/geh_sarnu.htm

---

[16] 47 Free Funeral Program Templates

https://templatelab.com/funeral-programs/

NOTES

8. Bibliography

Most Sacred Texts of Major World Religions

Religions	Most Sacred Text(s)
Baha'i	The Seven Valleys and The Four Valleys
Buddhism	Tipitaka
Christianity	Christian Bible
Hinduism	The Vedas and The Upanishads
Islam	The Quran and The Hadiths
Jainism	The Agamas
Judaism	The Tanakh and The Talmud
Shintoism	Kojiki
Sikhism	Guru Granth Sahib
Taoism	Tao Te Ching
Wicca	The Book of Shadows
Zoroastrianism	The Avesta

NOTES

NOTES

NOTES

CPSIA information can be obtained
at www.ICGtesting.com
Printed in the USA
LVHW050446010222
709871LV00014B/1832